AN A-Z OF JRR TOLKIEN'S
—THE—
HOBBIT

AN A-Z OF JRR TOLKIEN'S

—THE—
HOBBIT

AN UNENDORSED
COLOURFUL AND CRITICAL GUIDE
CELEBRATING THE MOVIES

SARAH OLIVER

JOHN BLAKE

Published by John Blake Publishing Ltd,
3 Bramber Court, 2 Bramber Road,
London W14 9PB, England

www.johnblakepublishing.co.uk

www.facebook.com/Johnblakepub   facebook

twitter.com/johnblakepub   twitter

First published in paperback in 2012

ISBN: 978 1 85782 955 6

British Library Cataloguing-in-Publication Data:

A catalogue record for this book is available from the British Library.

Design by www.envydesign.co.uk

Printed and bound by CPI Group (UK) Ltd

1 3 5 7 9 10 8 6 4 2

Papers used by John Blake Publishing are natural, recyclable products made
from wood grown in sustainable forests. The manufacturing processes
conform to the environmental regulations of the country of origin.

Every attempt has been made to contact the relevant copyright-holders,
but some were unobtainable. We would be grateful if the a
ppropriate people could contact us.

Dedicated with love to Mike,
Claire, Sarah and Barney.

Alfrid

Alfrid was a new character created by director Peter Jackson for *The Hobbit* movies. Through his Facebook page, Jackson told fans: 'The Master's conniving civil servant, Alfrid, will be played by Ryan Gage. Ryan is a great young actor who we originally cast in a small role, but we liked him so much, we promoted him to the much larger Alfrid part.'

Alfrid is Ryan's biggest movie role to date. Previously, he has worked mainly on the stage, appearing in several productions for the Royal Shakespeare Company. He has had small parts in the British TV shows *Hollyoaks*, *Doctors* and *The Bill*. Ryan trained at the Drama Centre London and graduated in 2005. He was performing in a Tom Stoppard play called *Artist Descending a Staircase* in a room over a pub when spotted by a casting assistant for *The Hobbit*. Originally he was cast as Drogo Baggins, but he impressed everyone so much that he was given the part of Alfrid.

Before making the trip to New Zealand to start filming *The Hobbit* Ryan played Simon H. Rifkind in *Ghost Stories* at the Duke of York's Theatre in London. On 16 July 2011, he tweeted: 'Tonight was the last *Ghost Stories* after 13 months in the West End. A big thank you to everyone who came to watch the show. #ghoststories.' However, he didn't have much time off as he had to be in New Zealand two weeks later. His first week on set was hectic, during which he tweeted: 'I've had a fun first week but I'm looking forward to getting some deep sleeping done this weekend.'

If you would like to follow Ryan on Twitter, his account is @RyanGage.

Peter Jackson, the director of *The Hobbit* movies, was thrilled that Ryan, and the other members of the cast and crew, got on really well as a team. He told News.com.au: 'Everybody's gotten to know each other very, very well and the spirit's great. I just believe when you're shooting a movie to have the atmosphere on set be friendly, and focused on the work, but have some fun.

'It's a long time to be getting up early in the morning and working 'til late at night – and if you're not enjoying it, you're not going to make a good film. There has to be a spirit on set amongst the cast and the crew that will ultimately rub off on the screen. We're having fun.'

Auditions

Thousands of people auditioned for parts in *The Hobbit*, including some famous faces. Boyzone star and Australian *X Factor* judge Ronan Keating was keen to win a part because he wants to become known as an actor as well as a singer. The first auditions took place in 2010.

Ronan told Clickonline.com: 'When a singer tries to become an actor it's very, very difficult. It's harder for someone, like a singer, to prove they can be an actor because people immediately want to say, "Oh, he's no good."

'I've gone to a lot of auditions over the years, and I've just never been ready, and I have never been good enough. But I feel over the last two years, I've grown into my skin and feel comfortable to prove to people that I can act.'

For his audition for *The Hobbit*, Ronan read for the part of an elf warrior but didn't manage to secure the part.

He is still glad he went for it, though, as it was a great opportunity — he thinks his lack of experience may have counted against him. Since his *Hobbit* audition he successfully auditioned for a part in an Australian movie called *Goddess* (March 2013) and was given the role of James Dickens, the main love interest.

He told journalist Kathryn Rogers: 'I wish the timing had been different and *Goddess* had come out before *The Hobbit* opportunity — maybe they would have given me the chance as it would have been an amazing film, and I would have been honoured to be involved.'

DID YOU KNOW?

British comedian and actor Bill Bailey auditioned unsuccessfully to play Glóin.

Comedian Jarred Christmas also auditioned for *The Hobbit* but he, too, was unsuccessful. He told Spoonfed.co.uk: 'Last year I auditioned for *The Hobbit*, to play one of the dwarves. I thought I could do it in my Kiwi accent but the casting guy wanted me to do it in a British accent. I started off West Country, went a little bit Welsh and ended in Cockney. I didn't get the part. I don't think they were after an accent-schizophrenic dwarf.'

Both Ronan and Jarred auditioned for speaking parts but there were hundreds of extra roles up for grabs.

Casting bosses decided to hold open auditions in Lower Hutt near Wellington, New Zealand, to find the extras they needed, but so many people turned up that they had to call the police. They had naively expected no more than 1,200 people but the number ended up being 3,000-plus.

Although the first 800 were allowed to audition, they then had to stop before things got out of control. The audition queue grew ridiculously long, crowd wrangler Chris Ryan explained to the *New Zealand Herald*: 'It was just starting to cause a few problems on the motorway, people slowing down and looking at the crowds really, I think more than anything else.

'The crowds were pretty good, most of them were pretty sensible and had set up; they brought umbrellas and chairs and sunblock.'

So many people wanted to be part of *The Hobbit* movie, and all sorts turned up. The official casting call had asked for men under 5'4" (163 cm), women under 5' (155 cm), big men with character faces 5'9" and over (175 cm-plus), men with large biceps of any height, women with character faces and long hair, men and women elves slim, athletic, 5'5"–6'4" (165–193 cm).

The decision was made to do the rest of the auditions online rather than face-to-face, to prevent the same thing from happening again.

Azog

- Name: Azog
- Alias: None
- Race: Orc (Goblin)
- Played by: John Rawls
- Character description: Azog is the King of the Orcs of Moria. He has a huge head and is a ferocious warrior. He doesn't actually appear in the book version of *The Hobbit*, but fans were thrilled when they found out he would be in a flashback scene in *The Hobbit* movies.

The actor chosen to play Azog was John Rawls, who trained at the EADA Academy of Dramatic Art in London and New Zealand. He has appeared in movies, plays, TV shows, music videos and commercials in New Zealand and in the UK. John is very skilled in stage combat (armed and unarmed), which helped him a great deal when playing Azog. He is a keen musician, his instruments being the guitar and trombone. In his spare time, he likes to rollerblade and writes scripts.

John is best known for playing Zurial in *30 Days of Night* (2007) and Hell Rider in the 2010 movie, *The Warrior's Way*. In April 2012, when it was announced that he would be playing Azog, fans were left feeling confused because Peter Jackson had written on his Facebook page back in May 2011 that Conan Stevens had been cast in the part. He wrote: 'Last, and certainly not least, is Conan Stevens, who will be playing an Orc called Azog (Orcs are never called Roger or Dennis for some strange reason). And yes that's his name – Conan! Isn't that cool? Azog is played by Conan! Here's a photo of Conan and I together. I'm pretty tall, probably at least 6'5" or 6'6" I would guess, so that gives you some clue how tall Conan is!'

It was then reported that it had been 'misinformation' first time around and instead Conan would be playing Bolg. Fans writing on online forums suggest that Peter had been right initially but that Conan had been promoted to Bolg because it is a bigger part, so that's why John replaced him.

Bain

- Name: Bain
- Race: Man of Dale
- Played by: John Bell
- Character description: Bain is the son of Bard the Bowman and becomes king after his father.

The actor chosen to play Bain was 13-year-old John Bell from Paisley in Scotland. He is best known for playing orphan Toby Coleman in the second series of *Tracy Beaker Returns* (2010) and Angus in the 2011 movie *Battleship*.

John's first acting job was in a play in Glasgow when he

was seven years old. The thing he finds the most fun about being an actor is getting to travel and meeting new people, but he dislikes being told he's been unsuccessful after auditioning for a part he really wants to play. John's favourite book is Kazuo Ishiguro's *Never Let Me Go*, his favourite TV show is *Glee* and his favourite band is Iron Maiden. When filming *The Hobbit*, he had to have a tutor so he didn't miss out on school. His classmates at home are really supportive and couldn't wait to see him in the movie.

When John was listed in an official press release as being a member of *The Hobbit* ensemble cast, fans were a bit confused because they had never heard of him. Hollywood Teen'Zine managed to track John down before anyone else and asked him about the role he would be playing. He said: 'I have just finished filming a small part in the film *Battleship* in Louisiana and I am about to start another project that I can't say anything about just yet. I have been offered a part in *The Hobbit* … my character is confident and brave and ready to do battle if required, even though he is still a boy. I have read *The Hobbit* and loved it, and I love Peter Jackson's *The Lord of the Rings* films, so you can definitely call me a fan.'

They also asked him to reveal a bit about himself and he said: 'I am 13 years old and have been acting since I was 7. I have been in *Doctor Who* in the UK and several other British programmes. *Shine of Rainbows* is my first feature film. I play the trumpet, drums and keyboard. I enjoy snowboarding and cycling and going to the cinema with my friends.'

John got his big break by entering a *Blue Peter* competition, which gave him the opportunity to act in an episode of *Doctor Who* alongside David Tennant. The actor he really rates is Jack Nicholson and his favourite film is *The Shining* – a strange choice for someone his age as it's a 15-rated horror movie!

Eagle-eyed fan Gaer Carreg was the first to suggest that John would be playing Bain as he had noticed some tweets going from John's official Twitter to Luke Evans' official Twitter. John had tweeted on 6 October '@Mr_Luke_Evans thanks Da! Happy now! See you soon. X'

Luke (Bard) had replied: '@johnbell123 no problem son! See you soon back in NZ.'

Balin
• Name: Balin
• Alias: Balin, Lord of Moria; Balin, Son of Fundin
• Race: Dwarf of the House of Durin
• Played by: Ken Stott
• Character description: Balin wears a red hood and looks very old. The brother of Dwalin, he is the second oldest dwarf on the quest. He was also the

second dwarf to arrive at Bilbo's home and is the dwarf usually given the job of lookout.

The actor chosen to play Balin was Ken Stott. Ken was born in Edinburgh, Scotland to his Sicilian mother, Antonia Sansica, and Scottish father. His dad was assistant head at the school that Ken was to attend. While growing up, Ken loved both music and acting and was a member of a band called Keyhole. Years after they split, his former bandmates formed the Bay City Rollers.

Ken trained at the Mountview Academy of Theatre Arts in London, but this hindered him when he tried to get acting jobs in Scotland. Struggling to earn enough money to live on, he supplemented his acting income with a second job as a double glazing salesman. He might have struggled at the beginning of his career but he is now one of the most-loved Scottish actors. Ken is best known for playing Detective Chief Inspector Red Metcalfe in *Messiah*, Detective Inspector Pat Chappel in *The Vice* and Adolf Hitler in *Uncle Adolf*.

DID YOU KNOW?

Ken's voice was used for Trufflehunter the badger in *The Chronicles of Narnia: Prince Caspian* (2008).

Ken is a consummate professional and in March 2009

stopped a performance of the play *A View from the Bridge* when schoolchildren in the audience started making lots of noise. An audience member later wrote on the What's On Stage website: 'From where I was sitting, I wasn't too aware of them – I definitely did hear them giggling at a few inappropriate moments, though. Since they were in the front row, I'm sure they must have been really irritating to the cast. His performance is so incredible and must require such a level of concentration that it is totally fair of him not to tolerate distractions like that.

'Their teacher was arguing that they hadn't done anything, and the ushers were trying their best to sort things out, and people in the audience were indeed getting quite rowdy and rebellious. It was all a bit uncomfortable. There were so many schoolchildren there and they were pretty silent after that little incident.'

DID YOU KNOW?

When Ken and his fellow dwarf actors were moving around on location they would quite often sit on an open-topped trailer together and be pulled along by a tractor.

Ken was thrilled to film *The Hobbit* in New Zealand as he revealed in the first dwarves' press conference: 'The credentials to shooting here are really second to none. It's not just because it's the spiritual home, you could say, for the piece but simply because it has fantastic facilities – the envy of the rest of the world.'

At the same press conference Mark Hadlow (Dori) said: 'It's an amazing experience as a theatre actor, when you've been an admirer for years, as I have been, of Ken Stott's work on stage and screen. To meet with him and get to talk about all the things that we share, has been extraordinary.'

Bard

- Name: Bard
- Alias: Bard the Bowman, Bard the Dragon-shooter, King Bard
- Race: Man of Dale
- Played by: Luke Evans
- Character description: Bard has long black hair and is the captain of a group of archers. After he kills Smaug the dragon, he becomes a great leader. He is a Man of Lake-town.

Luke Evans was chosen to play Bard. He is a Welsh actor, having been born in Pontypool and raised in Crumlin, a small village in Newbridge. Luke moved to Cardiff when he was seventeen years old to be coached by singing tutor

Louise Ryan. In 1997, he moved to London after he won a scholarship for The London Studio Centre. He graduated in 2000 and has been performing on the West End stage ever since. In 2008, he got his big break when cast as Vincent in the play *Small Change* at the Donmar Warehouse. He received rave reviews and came to the attention of casting directors and agents from the USA; he was also nominated for Best Newcomer in the *Evening Standard* Awards and then a couple of years later, was nominated for a 2011 National Movie Award in the category One to Watch.

DID YOU KNOW?

Luke was thirty years old when he auditioned for his first movie.

Because Luke's character doesn't appear until the second movie (2013) he didn't start filming at the same time as Martin Freeman and the dwarf actors. He also had to wait longer for his script to arrive. Luke confessed to *Empire Magazine*: 'I think what's been great about what Peter's doing online at the moment is doing these video blogs, which are just brilliant because for somebody who's not joined the cast at the beginning of the film, it's quite nice that by the time I do join it, I'm going to know who the actors are, who the roles are; I'm not going to be daunted by turning up in Middle-earth.'

He found walking around Bilbo's home the strangest experience because he remembered the first time he had seen it in the cinema when he was twenty-one. Back then he had no idea that he would be acting in a Tolkien movie.

Being cast as Bard was life changing for Luke – he had to leave London behind and move to New Zealand for a year. He says it's been the best job he's ever had, he's had an absolute blast and made some lifelong friends. Luke told MTV: 'Living in New Zealand, it's like a different world – it *is* a different world. It's very, very cool.

'We're so far away from home. We have a little family. Peter [Jackson] and the team create a very warm atmosphere, on set and off set. We all socialise, it's really special – I just feel very lucky to be a part of it.'

Initially, Luke was a bit jealous of the members of the cast who had been in *The Lord of the Rings* movies. He confessed to Collider.com: 'I feel very lucky to be here, you know – I'm watching this being made, and then watching Pete do his thing – because you only have to read any articles about the boys who were in the first three movies and how they talked about the experience being in New Zealand and working with Pete and the long period of time that you spent here.

'I was just very jealous of them, in a healthy way, but it was always something I was envious of. And now I'm here, and now I'm actually one of those boys – I'll always remember this as one of those experiences in my life.'

Luke thinks the hardest thing will be the return to normality as he has loved playing Bard so much. And he is so glad that director Peter Jackson decided to be faithful to the book, as he explained to Q TV at the British Film Awards: 'It's very loyal to the book. When you have a book like *The Hobbit*, you don't really need to embellish it much. The characters are so well written and everybody who loves the book will absolutely love this.'

Beorn

- Name: Beorn
- Alias: Skin-changer
- Race: Man
- Played by: Mikael Persbrandt
- Character description: Beorn is a skin-changer – he can change from a huge man to a black bear. His past is a bit of a mystery. He lives in a house on the edge of the mountains near the Carrock with his servants, who are animals with the ability to talk. The orcs killed the rest of his race.

When Guillermo del Toro was the director he had planned for *Hellboy* actor Ron Perlman to play Beorn and had written the part with him in mind. Ron had been planning on doing it, but once Guillermo stepped down, the casting changed. (*See* 'Delays' for more information on what happened.)

DID YOU KNOW?

For a while Guillermo del Toro had thought that Ron would be the perfect Smaug.

In the end, the actor chose to play Beorn was Mikael Persbrandt. When he was cast, Peter Jackson issued a press release, in which he stated: 'The role of Beorn is an iconic one and Mikael was our first choice for the part. Since seeing him read for the role we can't imagine anyone else playing this character.'

Mikael was born in Jakobsberg, Stockholms län, Sweden. A sporty child, he enjoyed football and boxing. He also liked building things and thought he would like to be an astronaut when he grew up. As he entered his teens, his career ambitions changed: he thought he wanted to become a dancer and joined the Academy of Ballet. After finishing his studies there, he caught the acting bug. His first role was as an extra in a production of *King Lear* at the Kungliga Dramatiska Teatern (Royal Dramatic Theatre) in Stockholm. He continued acting in plays before joining the cast of

Swedish soap opera *Rederiet* in 1992. In 1999, Mikael was nominated for the Guldbagge Award for Best Leading Actor – a huge achievement. Following this, he quickly became one of Sweden's finest actors. Mikael gained international fame when he played Anton in the Susanne Bier movie *In a Better World*, which won the Best Foreign Language Film at the 2011 Oscars. Usually, he plays tough characters.

DID YOU KNOW?

In the past, Mikael Persbrandt has worked as a taxi driver.

Securing the role of Beorn was a dream come true for Mikael as he had loved reading Tolkien's books when he was a child (he used to visit bookshops in the hope of finding early editions). He must have been very keen to see the script for the first *Hobbit* movie, but this was kept under wraps until it was almost time for filming to begin. To start with, he was given only five pages of script and he had to sign to say that he had received them. No one wanted the script to get out because it would ruin the surprises Peter Jackson had in store for the fans.

On his first day on set Mikael was surprised how it felt to play Beorn, even though he had spent a long time preparing how he was going to play the character. He had to do a scene which involved him being hoisted high into the air in the studio where King Kong was filmed. It was a tough scene to do, and Mikael felt a bit awkward at first but he was soon made to feel at ease. Peter Jackson is a director who is willing to take on board his actors thoughts on their characters so Mikael was able to share his thoughts.

Before moving to New Zealand in 2011, he trained at the Swedish Nacka Martial Arts Centre, but once he arrived, he had training sessions with the rest of the cast. He trained six days a week and when he wasn't in the gym, he would be cycling miles at a time on his mountain bike. As well as training his body to be physically ready to play Beorn, he had to have language lessons because his understanding of English was very limited to begin with.

DID YOU KNOW?

Mikael Persbrandt did some of his training under the instruction of the Navy Seals.

Mikael is a man who likes to make a difference and he was a Swedish UNICEF Goodwill Ambassador for six years. He has visited children living in Brazilian slums, child soldiers in Liberia, children in Haiti after the 2010 earthquake and been on many trips at home and abroad to raise the profile of UNICEF.

Bert

- Name: Bert
- Alias: Liar, Lout
- Race: Stone-troll
- Played by: Not cast yet (likely to be CGI – computer generated imagery)
- Character description: Bert, William and Tom are trolls and spend their time eating anyone who passes their way on the road west of Rivendell.

> **DID YOU KNOW?**
> Tolkien's children loved the stone-trolls and wished they hadn't been turned to stone!

When fans discussed who they would like to voice Bert on *The Hobbit Movie Forum*, popular choices included Robin Williams, Vinnie Jones and Bob Hoskins. Others believed actors who had already appeared in *The Lord of the Rings* movies should play Bert, William and Tom.

Bifur

- Name: Bifur
- Alias: None
- Race: Dwarf of Khazad-dûm (not of Durin's line)
- Played by: William Kircher

- Character description: Bifur is the brother of Bombur and the cousin of Bofur. He wears a yellow hood and joins the quest to get a share in the treasure. He is descended from ironworkers and coal miners from the West, not from the Longbeard Dwarves of the House of Durin. He plays the clarinet and is fond of apple tart!

The actor chosen to play Bifur was William Kircher, who is hugely popular in New Zealand. His professional acting career started when he graduated from the New Zealand Drama School at the age of eighteen (he had been the youngest student in his class as he had lied about his age in order to get on the course). Since then he has acted in over 100 professional theatre productions, as well as appearing in numerous TV shows and movies. He has played several police officers over the years and quite a few bad guys, too.

William has also stepped the other side of the camera as a producer and television company executive. For years he refused to attend auditions and turned down jobs he was offered because he no longer wanted to act. This all changed when Robert Sarkies approached him for the 2006 movie *Out of the Blue*, based on the Aramoana Massacre. Up until that point he had thought that being a producer might be better than being an actor, but changed his mind after being offered the role of police officer Stu Guthrie, and after he had a disappointing experience at a conference. He explained to NZ on Screen: 'For some time I thought being a producer would be a more fulfilling career than being an actor but then I went to a conference in Cannes with 300 other producers, all desperately chasing finance for their projects and realised being an actor wasn't so bad after all!'

In his spare time William likes to spend time with his wife, Nicole Chesterman, a rock singer and talent agent, and their four daughters. They enjoy walking their dogs as a family and William loves fishing. He lives in Eastbourne in the southern North Island of New Zealand.

During one of the behind-the-scenes production videos, William discussed how the dwarf actors prepared before filming began. He said: 'We started with three months of intense training: we did stunt fighting, horse riding; we did the gym four times a week, we did dwarf movement intensely. They did it essentially by breaking us down, reducing us to the absolute ameba stage and then building us up again as dwarves.'

All the delays to filming at the start actually helped William and his new colleagues as it allowed them to spend more time training, and they also had more time to bond with each other. When in costume they had to carry 80 kg of props, plus the weight of their fat suits.

In the first *Hobbit* press conference, William admitted that *The Lord of the Rings* movies had set the bar high. 'We are all really focused on the work at this stage,' he said. 'We have a lot to live up to and are completely and utterly determined to live up to it.'

Bilbo Baggins

- Name: Bilbo Baggins
- Alias: Elf-friend, Ringbearer
- Race: Hobbit
- Played by: Martin Freeman and Ian Holm
- Character description: Bilbo is a stereotypical hobbit. Hobbits are jolly, little people, roughly half the size of humans. Clean-shaven, they are smaller than dwarves. They have hairy feet with leathery soles and they dress in yellow and green.

Bilbo is the main character in *The Hobbit* and becomes a hero adventurer after a wizard called Gandalf calls by his hobbit-hole. Although not interested in adventure, Bilbo ends up being given the job of burglar and goes on a quest with 13 dwarves.

Several actors have played Bilbo in the past. In *The Lord of the Rings* trilogy he was played by Ian Holm and in the 1977 animated version of *The Hobbit*, Orson Bean took on the role. Orson also played Bilbo in the 1980 animated version of *The Return of the King*.

The actor chosen by Peter Jackson to play Bilbo in his *Hobbit* movies was Martin Freeman. In a statement released to the press, Peter said: 'Despite the various rumours and speculation surrounding this role, there has only ever been one Bilbo Baggins for us.

'There are few times in your career when you come across an actor who you know was born to play a role, but that was the case as soon as I met Martin. He is intelligent, funny, surprising and brave – exactly like Bilbo, and I feel incredibly proud to be able to announce that he is our Hobbit.'

Before being cast in *The Hobbit* Martin was best known in the UK for playing Dr John Watson in *Sherlock* and Tim in *The Office*. In the USA he was best known for his part in the movie *Love Actually* (2003), but as soon as he was cast as Bilbo that all changed. Back in January 2012, he admitted to talk show host Graham Norton: 'I have had ten years to prepare since *The Office*, but we were on holiday recently and I realised that maybe this time next year there won't be many places where I can go where *The Hobbit* won't have been seen. It's a funny thing [fame] and I have a troubled relationship with that sort of stuff.'

Martin had auditioned for one of Peter Jackson's past movies, *The Lovely Bones* (2009). He had wanted to play the murderer George Harvey but Stanley Tucci got the part instead. At the time he was gutted, but it really was a blessing in disguise: had he been successful, he might not have been able to play Bilbo because people would have associated him with that role.

Initially, he actually had to turn down the part of Bilbo because he was already committed to playing Watson in the second series of the BBC drama *Sherlock*, but he did say that if something could be done with the timings, then he would like to be involved. Because of the various filming delays in the months that followed, it turned out that he was able to take on the role as he could film *Sherlock* in the gaps. He explained what happened in a New Zealand press conference in early 2011: 'I put myself on tape for it early last year and I'd always had very generous feedback from the team that they would like me to do it ultimately, which was a very nice vote of confidence and certainly relaxed me a bit. I thought I was not going to be able to do it because of other commitments in Britain then it was made that I could do it. So yeah, it's genuinely flattering and it means that I get to do two things [*The Hobbit* and *Sherlock*] that I really love this year.'

DID YOU KNOW?

David Tennant, James McAvoy and Tobey Maguire had all been considered for the role of Bilbo.

If Peter Jackson had to liken himself to any character from Middle-earth, he would pick Bilbo. As he explained to Sasha Stone from the *Mirror*: 'I really should identify with a sword-wielding hero like Aragorn [from *The Lord of the Rings*] but really, I identify more with a comfort-loving hobbit like Bilbo Baggins, who would rather put his feet up in front of the fire and eat cakes and drink ale, and not go on any adventures and lead a quiet life.'

Martin Freeman is a British actor, originally from Aldershot, Hampshire, England. He trained at the Central School of Speech & Drama in London and is a versatile actor, having appeared in numerous TV shows, theatre productions, movies and radio shows. Best known for playing Arthur Dent in *The Hitchhiker's Guide to the Galaxy* (2005), Tim in the UK version of *The Office* and Dr Watson in the TV series *Sherlock*, he won a 2011 BAFTA TV Award for playing Dr Watson (picking up the Best Supporting Actor Award). This has been his biggest accolade to date, but his performances in *The Hobbit* movies could see him win an Oscar or Golden Globe in the future.

Martin was told initially that he would have to be in New Zealand for 18 months straight but that wouldn't have been practical for him because he has a family. In the end, he had to juggle filming *The Hobbit* movies with episodes of *Sherlock*, which wasn't easy but allowed him to go back to the UK to see his two young children. Thankfully his partner Amanda Abbington understands what it is like because she is an actress, too. Though unmarried, they frequently call each other husband and wife and are happy as they are with their two children, two dogs and a cat.

When filming in New Zealand, Amanda told *Daily Mail* journalist Vicki Power: 'When he'd been out there for over six weeks, he really needed to see us. His heart ached a little bit. But we know the film is going to be huge.

'He does get stressed, though. Sometimes he rings me up at 7 am to say: "I've been covered in c★★p, hanging upside down and I've got bloody ears on." But he knows it's for the greater good and he does it with a smile.'

Peter Jackson is so glad Martin took on the role. He told fansshare.com: 'He is fantastic and there is simply nobody else for the job. We couldn't find anyone who was better than him. He is simply fantastic.

'He's Bilbo-esque. You might not always want to say that about you, right? But seriously he has the essential features of this little English gent, this country gent who is slightly old-fashioned and has to go around in the world and try to cope with it.

'That's not exactly who Martin is as a person, but as an actor he does that so well – the fish out of water with a sense of courage but also a wonderful sense of humour.

The things that happen to him and the way he reacts to them – things he's never seen in his life before as a stuffy little Hobbit – his response to it all is part of the charm. And he does have a great openness in his face.'

Playing an upbeat hobbit was hard work on the days when Martin was covered in mud and there were long days filming, too.

Sir Ian Holm played the older Bilbo in *The Hobbit* movies and in *The Lord of the Rings* trilogy. Born in Goodmayes, London to Scottish parents, he trained at the Royal Academy of Dramatic Art, graduating in 1953, and then worked in Stratford becoming one of the lead actors in the Royal Shakespeare Company. Throughout the fifties and sixties he performed in numerous Shakespeare plays in the UK and USA before appearing in his first movie, *The Bofor's Gun* (1968). The part of Flynn earned him a BAFTA for Best Supporting Actor. Throughout his long career, Ian has been nominated for over 30 different awards and, altogether, picked up 19 of them – quite an achievement. One of the finest actors the UK has ever produced, he has previously been nominated for an Oscar but that was back in 1982 for *Chariots of Fire*, so he is well overdue another nomination.

During a press conference before shooting began, Martin was asked how he would be playing Bilbo. He replied: 'Obviously I've been looking at what he [Ian] was doing;

there's a certain level of course of which I have to match what he's doing and then forget it as well so I've not been tying myself in knots about it but I have been trying to be sensible and just literally look at what he's doing, what his voice is doing, what his movements are doing. And I genuinely, without being bigheaded or falsely modest, I think I'm quite a good match for him. I've seen worse matches and I think I can do a young Ian Holm. So I'm looking forward to it, but bearing in mind that I can't be playing Ian Holm, you know what I mean. But of course I'm going to have that echoing and nod to what he did.'

Ian filmed his scenes and close-ups for *The Hobbit* in England rather than coming all the way to New Zealand, so Martin actually stood in for him in a scene with Elijah Wood (Frodo). Before they began shooting, Jackson and his crew watched the footage that Ian had done in London so they could easily match up the shots. *Hobbit* superfan Eric Vespe got to witness what happened and wrote in his report for AintItCool.com: 'While I didn't talk to Elijah about it, I bet it meant the world to him to have Martin there actually giving a performance for him to act off of. Freeman even adopted a little bit of Ian Holm's speech patterns for these scenes and was so good at impersonating Ian Holm that more than once I wondered if the voice I was hearing over the coms was Ian's on playback or Martin's in real life.

'Usually in these situations they'll have the script girl or one of the dialect coaches read the lines and while that works a charm, there's something extra special about a performer giving a performance.'

DID YOU KNOW?

While filming in Hobbiton one of the cow extras decided it didn't want to be in the movie anymore and so it ran off! A crewmember had to run after it and the scene was reshot.

Birmingham

J.R.R. Tolkien, author of *The Hobbit*, may have been born in Bloemfontein in the Orange Free State (known today as Free State Province, South Africa), but tourism bosses in Birmingham, England are keen to point out that from 1895 to 1911 he lived in the city. His grandparents owned a shop in the centre, which had been in the family since the early 1800s (the building it was situated in was called Lamb House). Tolkien's great-great-grandfather had run a stationer's and bookshop from Lamb House and following this, his great grandfather had a drapery and hosiery store there.

Birmingham tourism bosses are hoping that *The Hobbit* movies will bring tourists to the city to see where Tolkien spent his childhood and witness for themselves the buildings that are said to have inspired Tolkien while writing. It is thought that the Two Towers from *The Lord of the Rings* are based on Perrott's Folly and Edgbaston Waterworks. Perrott's Folly is nicknamed 'The Observatory' and is a 29 m-high tower. Built in 1758, it is Grade II listed.

Local volunteer Chris Hoare told Darren Cannan from the BBC during a trip to Perrott's Folly in 2003: 'Don't forget Tolkien lived at 25 Stirling Road, went to the Oratory and drank in the Ivy Bush.'

Tourism bosses have recently opened a new Tolkien themed gallery at Sarehole Mill in Hall Green, which shows *The Hobbit* author's links with Birmingham through photographs and film. Chairman of the Birmingham Tolkien Group Michael Wilkes is overjoyed with the gallery and told Neil Elkes from the *Birmingham Mail*: 'This is a step forward for Tolkien heritage in Birmingham. The Birmingham Tolkien Group has worked closely with the city museum service on this. We get visitors from all over the world here and we've even had visitors from Eastern Europe.'

As well as the gallery, the city has held a Tolkien weekend every year since 2000. The 2012 weekend celebrated 75 years since *The Hobbit* was published. It was called 'Middle-earth Weekend' and took place at Shire County Park on 19 and 20 May. There were re-enactments of key scenes from Tolkien's books, medieval craftsmen, archery, dancing, music and much more. It was a free event and people travelled from far and wide to take part.

Bofur

- Name: Bofur
- Alias: None
- Race: Dwarf of Khazad-dûm (not of Durin's line)
- Played by: James Nesbitt
- Character description: Bofur wears a yellow hood and is the brother of Bombur, cousin of Bifur.

The actor chosen to play Bofur was James Nesbitt. James, or 'Jimmy' as he likes to be called, is originally from Ballymena, County Antrim, Northern Ireland. At thirteen, he made his stage debut playing the Artful Dodger in *Oliver Twist*. Although he dreamed of being a French teacher, he changed his mind while at university and dropped out of the course, having decided that he would much rather become an actor, and enrolled at the Central School of Speech & Drama in London.

James talked to Stuff.co.nz about why he changed his career ambitions, saying: 'I got fed up writing essays and I'd done a bit of acting, so I packed in the degree. Drama school was a really good way of meeting girls [laughs] but then I started work the day after I left drama school and all of a sudden it was like "OK, I'm an actor".

'I think I was very lucky that I came from Northern Ireland at a time when a lot of drama was coming out of there because of the conflict. I remember (on my first day's work), I got 250 quid a day (which is still bloody good money) and this was 1988. You see there's an old Protestant work ethic in me: I don't mind earning a few quid. And so I thought, "Right, I'll stick with this." '

He graduated in 1987 and began his career acting in plays and musicals before securing the part of talent agent Fintan O'Donnell in the 1991 movie *Hear My Song*. James is most famous for playing Adam Williams in the smash hit TV comedy–drama series *Cold Feet* (1997–2003) and Tommy Murphy in the TV drama *Murphy's Law*. He has been nominated for over 20 awards, including a Golden Globe in 2008 for his portrayal of Tom Jackman in the TV series *Jekyll*. So far he has picked up eight awards, from a British Comedy Award to a British Independent Film Award, and from an Irish Film and Television Award to a Stockholm Film Festival Award.

In a press release to announce that James had been cast as Bofur, Peter Jackson said: 'James's charm, warmth and wit are legendary, as is his range as an actor in both comedic and dramatic roles. We feel very lucky to be able to welcome him as one of our cast.'

> **FILM FACT:**
>
> James Nesbitt (aside from Billy Connolly) is arguably the funniest member of *The Hobbit* cast. He has never done stand-up, but has the cast and crew in stitches with some of the things he says.

James's family initially found moving to New Zealand a bit traumatic. His daughters Peggy (thirteen) and Mary (ten) didn't want to leave their friends behind in London and so it was tough on them. James admitted at a Wellington press conference: 'Kids at a certain age don't necessarily want to be dragged to the other side of the world, but they've certainly been made to feel very welcome; they are loving the schools.'

His daughters soon settled in and were hoping their dad could have a word with Peter Jackson and get them jobs as extras. James confessed this was one of the conditions they made when they agreed to move to New Zealand for a year. His biggest struggle now that he lives so far from home is getting up at the crack of dawn to watch his horse (Riverside Theatre) at the races or to see Manchester United play.

James is married to the actress Sonia Forbes-Adam. The film company hired them a gorgeous house in Wellington to live in while James was filming. They arrived in New

Zealand just before the Christchurch earthquake. James talked about what it was like to the *Daily Mail*, confiding: 'When we first arrived it was so tranquil and calm that we relaxed immediately, but since the earthquake it has been a strange time. Wellington itself was unaffected, but a number of the crew and cast know people in Christ-church, and the whole country is in a state of shock.

'It's such a terrible thing to happen and it's dominated the news every day, so it can't help but affect the atmosphere. People are pulling together and there is a real sense of resilience in the face of adversity.'

James enjoyed the dwarf training they had to do for weeks before filming started. He told Digital Spy what was involved: 'We're doing lots of horse riding and stunts and stuff. We're basically playing! It's a very good way to earn a living; it's great. They're working us hard, I have to say but they're very down to earth. It has such a feeling of being a little company, it just happens to be a little company of thousands of people! But everyone is enjoying it. Every day's a little treat.'

He refused to say who was the worst pupil, instead choosing to say: 'Richard Armitage [Thorin] is very good at the old horse riding because of course he did it in *Robin Hood*, so he's very good at that. Of course he's playing our leader, so it's right that he's good at that. Aidan Turner (Kili) and Rob Kazinsky (Fili), they're fit young men. But we're all shapes and all sizes and we all have our own skills.'

There were 21 trailers used when filming *The Hobbit* and the cast each had one with their name on it. James decorated his trailer with a big New Zealand flag, coloured garlands, an Irish flag, plus ribbons in the Irish colours of green, white and orange. He had a framed photo of his dog and lots of pictures of home and the seaside in Ireland; he also had a photomontage of his racing horse, Riverside Theatre.

DID YOU KNOW?

A few weeks after arriving in New Zealand, James went to the Wellington Sevens rugby tournament dressed as a chicken! He revealed in the first *Hobbit* press conference: 'I was in the corporate box and I was the only one in costume. People were talking to me, obviously thinking, "He's supposed to be somebody [important] but he's a chicken." ' Why a chicken? His reply: 'It just felt right.'

Bolg

- Name: Bolg
- Alias: Bolg of the North
- Race: Orc (Goblin)

- Played by: Conan Stevens
- Character description: Bolg is an orc warlord. A typical goblin, he is cruel and uncaring.

The actor chosen to play Bolg was Australian actor Conan Stevens. He almost didn't get the part because he missed the first round of auditions as he didn't find out about them in time, but thankfully his manager was able to speak to the casting director. They arranged for Conan to film an audition and send it to the casting director via the Internet but, before he could do so, Conan contracted dysentery (an inflammatory disorder of the intestines) and so he was really sick. Because there was no time to waste and he didn't want to miss out, he had to film the audition even though he had lost a lot of weight and was feeling low on energy. The casting director was very impressed when he saw the audition and the rest is history.

Getting a part in *The Hobbit* movies meant so much to Conan because the book had had a huge impact on his life when he read it as a 12-year-old schoolboy. He loved it and went on to read *The Lord of the Rings*, *The Odyssey* and more books about Roman and Greek mythology. Following this, he then began role-playing games such as *Dungeon & Dragons*, *Aftermath* and *Warhammer*. By the time he was sixteen he had decided that he wanted to be an action movie star. To find out more about Conan, visit www.conanstevens.com.

Before being cast, Conan had spent 25 years as a professional wrestler and martial arts expert. He is a massive 7' ¼" tall, and prior to *The Hobbit* his biggest acting role was playing Gregor Clegane in the *Game of Thrones* TV series (2011).

In between filming the first and second *Hobbit* movies, Conan shot the *Spartacus* TV series in Auckland. He played a German character called Sedullus. This proved to be a big challenge because the majority of his lines were in German, a language he couldn't speak. He also squeezed in the movie *Vikingdom* (2012), which was filmed in Malaysia, playing the Nordic God of Thunder, Thor.

DID YOU KNOW?

As well as acting in films, Conan Stevens is a keen movie scriptwriter and has written four movie scripts to date.

It takes a lot of effort for Conan to look as ripped as he does and he has to work out a lot. He is such a big guy that he eats every two hours to make sure he has enough energy for when he hits the gym. Conan takes care with what he eats, and when filming *The Hobbit* he tried to consume as much organic, naturally grown vegetables, meat and eggs as possible.

Bombur

- Name: Bombur
- Alias: Poor fat Bombur
- Race: Dwarf of Khazad-dûm (not of Durin's line)
- Played by: Stephen Hunter
- Character description: Bombur is a huge, fat dwarf. Brother of Bofur and cousin of Bifur, he plays the drum and wears a pale green hood.

The actor chosen to play Bombur was New Zealand actor and voiceover artist, Stephen Hunter. Stephen plays mainly comedic characters in TV shows, having appeared in only one movie before being cast as Bombur. He is most famous for being in a Toyota ad with his top off and he doesn't mind being overweight: if he'd been slim, he wouldn't have been cast as Bombur.

Stephen started out acting in school plays and then he began recording radio ads before moving to Sydney seven years ago to become an actor. At first he stayed with friends before getting his own place. He found himself an agent and auditioned unsuccessfully for a role in *The Lord of the Rings*. To pay the bills, he started doing ads and voiceover jobs, but financially times were tough – he couldn't get a part-time job because he had to be available in case his agent rang with an acting job.

DID YOU KNOW?

Like many of the actors playing dwarves, Stephen had read *The Hobbit* as a child but he didn't get to read *The Lord of the Rings* trilogy until he was in his twenties – and it took him a year to get through it!

When Stephen was told about *The Hobbit* auditions he was excited but nearly messed up on the day because he followed a friend's advice and did some exercises before going in. He did some press-ups but felt out of breath and nearly didn't make it in. Once the audition was over, he had to wait a whole two months before he got the call telling him that he'd landed the part of Bombur. His pregnant partner Laura was at home at the time and she thought something bad had happened to someone they knew because Stephen went deathly pale with shock. There were so many famous actors lined up to be in *The Hobbit* movies and now he was about to rub shoulders with them!

Stephen admitted in Production Video 6: 'I think my favourite day on set unquestionably was floating down the Pelorus River in barrels. That was way cool and if they ever make that a ride, life-time pass, please!'

Another highlight was his very first day on set because he got to see Bilbo's hobbit home and do a walk-through with Jackson and the rest of the dwarves. When they were filming there the police arrived and warned them that they were about to issue a severe weather warning so they had to pack everything up as quickly as they could. It's a good job they did because just a few hours later, the whole area was flooded. The river water level rose approximately 20–30 feet!

Books

J.R.R. Tolkien, creator of *The Hobbit*, was an author, poet, university lecturer and philologist. His book, *The Hobbit*, is one of the world's bestselling books of all time. Its full title is *The Hobbit, or There and Back Again*. It was first published on 21 September 1937 and all 1,500 copies from the initial print run had sold by the December. The following year, it was released in America. It was a big hit, winning a Best Juvenile Fiction award from the *New York Tribune*, as well as being nominated for a prestigious Carnegie Medal. Over the years, it has won lots of other awards, too.

The book was published by George Allen & Unwin, who asked Tolkien to write a sequel in the December of that year; he sent them a draft of *The Silmarillion* but they wanted a book about hobbits instead. He then wrote *The*

Lord of the Rings between 1937 and 1949, but had to make changes to some aspects of *The Hobbit*, so a few more editions were published over the years. *The Lord of the Rings* books are less humorous and aimed at an older audience than *The Hobbit*.

Bravery, personal growth and war are the major themes in *The Hobbit*. Tolkien had experience of war having been a soldier in World War I. When writing *The Hobbit*, he was also influenced by fairy tales and Anglo-Saxon literature.

After leaving the army, he became a professor at Oxford University. Two of his poems were published; the first was called *The Car and the Fiddle: A Nursery Rhyme Undone and its Scandalous Secret Unlocked* and the second was *Goblin Feet*.

DID YOU KNOW?

Tolkien enjoyed sending his children letters from Father Christmas, but with his own unique slant. Often they included a polar bear, goblins and gnomes.

The story behind how J.R.R. Tolkien began writing *The Hobbit* is rather interesting. He was marking School Certificate papers in the early 1930s when out of the blue he decided to write 'In a hole in the ground there lived a hobbit' on a blank page. It wasn't until late 1932 when he had finished the story that he decided to send it to some of his friends for feedback. One such friend was C.S. Lewis, who wrote *The Lion, The Witch and the Wardrobe*. He also loaned a copy of the manuscript to one of his students, Elaine Griffiths.

In 1936, during a visit from Susan Dagnall from the publisher George Allen & Unwin, Elaine suggested that Susan read Tolkien's manuscript. She promptly did so and, suitably impressed, took it to her boss, Stanley Unwin. He enjoyed it but before making a decision, he handed it to his son Rayner, who was ten at the time. He gave it the thumbs-up and the rest is history.

As well as writing *The Hobbit*, all the dust jackets, maps and illustrations were designed by Tolkien, too. He knew precisely how he wanted *The Hobbit* to look and sent his publisher lots of letters before it was published. Rayner Unwin wrote in his publishing memoir: 'In 1937 alone Tolkien wrote 26 letters to George Allen & Unwin, detailed, fluent, often pungent, but infinitely polite and exasperatingly precise. I doubt any author today, however famous, would get such scrupulous attention.'

Tolkien's original dust jacket design had four colours but because of the associated costs, his publishers decided not to have a red sun.

DID YOU KNOW?

Tolkien found the epic poem *Beowulf* one of his 'most valued sources'. Several comparisons can be made between what happens in *The Hobbit* and what takes place in *Beowulf*.

Some scholars and Tolkien fans see *The Hobbit* as being a parable of the First World War. When directing the movies, Guillermo del Toro spent weeks doing as much research as he could on World War I to understand Tolkien's mindset. Some people think of *The Hobbit* and *The Lord of the Rings* books as being fantasy novels, but Peter Jackson confided in *Mirror* journalist Sasha Stone: 'Tolkien never thought he was making fantasy. He loved English sagas and the Norse sagas, and he found that England had lost its mythology.'

After *The Hobbit* was released, Tolkien's friend C.S. Lewis wrote in *The Times*: 'The truth is that in this book a number of good things, never before united, have come together: a fund of humour, an understanding of children, and a happy fusion of the scholar's with the poet's grasp of mythology. The professor has the air of inventing nothing. He has studied trolls and dragons at first hand and describes them with that fidelity that is worth oceans of glib "originality".'

W.H. Auden felt it was 'one of the best children's stories of this century.'

There have been many *Hobbit* adaptations over the years. The first stage adaptation took place in March 1953 at St Margaret's School, Edinburgh. It was performed by girls, which is rather strange as there are no female characters in the book. There was a BBC Radio 4 adaptation in 1968 and a year later the first movie adaptation came out (it was 12 minutes long, with cartoon stills). A comic-book adaptation was released in 1989 and the following year a one-volume edition was published. In 1977, an animated TV movie version was released and was nominated for the Hugo Award for Best Dramatic Presentation. In the past three decades, there have been numerous video and computer games based on *The Hobbit*.

It is thought that as many as 100 million copies of *The Hobbit* could have been sold since the very first print run in 1937. First editions are so highly sought after that a signed copy can go for over £60,000 ($94,212) at auction.

During an interview with *Rotten Tomatoes*, Guillermo del Toro summed up *The Hobbit* book. He said: 'It is a very different book than the trilogy. It is a book that is written from a start of innocence and an ending of disappointment. The ending of *The Hobbit* is quite bittersweet, quite melancholic in a way. The exposure of

Bilbo to the war is the exposure of a generation of English men to World War I.

'The reason why I connect with *The Hobbit* is because it's all seen from a really humble, honest, little guy point of view. I'm not saying Bilbo is a child, I don't think he is, but he is a very sheltered character and I love the journey.'

In an interview with *Total Film*, Peter Jackson and Fran Walsh also summed up *The Hobbit* and discussed how it differs from *The Lord of the Rings* books. Peter said: '*The Hobbit* is very much a children's book and *The Lord of the Rings* is something else; it's not really aimed at children at all. I realised the characters of the dwarves are the difference – their energy and disdain of anything politically correct brings a new kind of spirit to it. The dwarves give it a kind of childish, comedic quality that gives us a very different tone from *The Lord of the Rings* trilogy.'

Fran added: 'We always saw *The Hobbit* more in the golden light of a fairytale; it's more playful. But by the time you get to the end, Tolkien is writing himself into that place where he can begin that epic journey of writing *LOTR* [*Lord of the Rings*], which took, as he put it, his life's blood. All those heavier, darker themes which are so prevalent in the later trilogy start to come [more] into play in *There and Back Again*.'

DID YOU KNOW?

Guillermo del Toro read all of Tolkien's books on Middle-earth to prepare for writing and directing *The Hobbit*.

Although *The Hobbit* was written for children, both Guillermo del Toro and Peter Jackson believed that *The Hobbit* movies could be darker. During a live chat in 2008, Peter confessed to fans: 'I personally feel that *The Hobbit* can, and should have a different tone. The "tone" of these stories shouldn't be defined by the pressure our characters were under in *LOTR* – the world is a different place at the time of *The Hobbit*; the shadow is not so dark. However, what should stay the same is the reality of Middle-earth and the integrity we bring to it as filmmakers.'

Across the years, *The Hobbit* has been translated into over 50 languages, but more translations are being done even today. In May 2011, *The Hobbit* was published in the Irish language, much to the delight of fans. Irish Gaelic is a minority language but many classic books have been translated into it over time. When the *Harry Potter* books were launched in Irish Gaelic they proved to be a big hit but experts predicted that *An Hobad* (*The Hobbit*) would be the best-selling Irish language book ever. Fans are hoping *The Lord of the Rings* books will be next to be translated.

The book's launch was held at An Siopa Leabhar (The Book Shop) in Dublin and the experts who had the task of translating it, Professor Nicholas Williams and publisher Michael Everson, were on hand to answer questions.

DID YOU KNOW?

There is no word in Irish Gaelic to describe elves like the ones that feature in *The Hobbit* so they had to invent a new word: 'Ealbh'.

In September 2012, HarperCollins published a Latin version of *The Hobbit* called *Hobbitus Ille* to celebrate the book's 75th birthday. It was translated by Mark Walker and the publisher stated it was 'great for students learning Latin, but also for fans who want to dip in and find favourite passages.'

The first line reads 'In foramine terrae habitabat hobbitus' (In a hole in the ground, there lived a hobbit).

In April 2012, it was announced that Tolkien's oldest grandson – Michael Tolkien – was to release two fantasy books for children with Gerald Dickens, the great-great grandson of Charles Dickens. Michael Tolkien is a keen poet and critic, having retired from teaching in 1994. He was born in Birmingham and the two books will be based on stories read to him as a child by Tolkien. Gerald Dickens will narrate the audio book versions. The first book is called *Wish* and was influenced by the 1923

Florence Bone tale, *The Rose-Coloured Wish*. *Rainbow* is the second book and is again influenced by the work of Florence Bone, only this time by her story, *The Other Side of the Rainbow*.

Tolkien fans are hoping that *The Hobbit* movies will inspire people to pick up a copy of the book and read it for themselves rather than just enjoy the films, because although they are said to be true to the book, there are differences. On 25 March each year it is Tolkien Reading Day, a joint venture by the Tolkien Society and fan site TheOneRing to encourage people to pick up a classic Tolkien book and read it.

Chief of the Guards

- Name: Chief of the Guards
- Alias: The guard, Turnkey
- Race: Elf of the Woodland Realm
- Played by: Not yet cast
- Character description: Mirkwood elves are usually golden haired with bright eyes. They are 6' tall or more and wear green and brown clothing. The Chief of the Guards is a friend of the King's Butler. He works in the dungeons and is fond of wine.

Chief Wolf

- Name: Chief Wolf
- Alias: Hound of Sauron
- Race: Wolves of the North, Wargs of Wilderland
- Played by: N/A
- Character description: A big, grey wolf, he communicates with his fellow Wargs using their own language. The Wargs and the goblins often worked together on raids and shared the treasure. They enjoy doing evil and wicked things. Although pretty unbeatable, the Wargs do hate fire.

Long before Guillermo del Toro stepped down as director, he told the *New Yorker* in an interview: 'There will be different sensibilities involved in this movie than there were in the original trilogy. First of all, because we have the travelogues in *The Hobbit*, which goes to places and variations on races that were not addressed in the trilogy. My belief on the "Wargs" issue is that the classical incarnation of the demonic wolf in Nordic mythology is not a hyena-shaped creature: it is a wolf. The archetype is a wolf, so we're going to go back to the slender, archetypical wolf that is, I think, the inspiration for Tolkien.'

In a webchat with fans he stated that the Wargs: '...will be different from the Hyena ones established in the

Trilogy; they will be faithful to the creatures in the book and will be redesigned accordingly.'

CinemaCon

The Official Convention of The National Association of Theatre Owners, CinemaCon, takes place at Caesars Palace, Las Vegas in March/April time. For *Hobbit* fans, the 2012 event was extra-special as an exclusive preview of the movie was to be given.

The audience were told by an onscreen Peter Jackson to put on their 3D glasses and following this, he briefly talked about the history of movies and how different frame rates were introduced when the move away from silent films was made. He explained that for the past 70 years moviegoers had been seeing films with a standard 24 frames-per-second, but that *The Hobbit* would be showing at 48 frames-per-second. The preview of 10 minutes then started.

Quickbeam from TheOneRing.net wrote in his review: 'For a breathless moment I felt rather like someone in an audience seeing their first color film after endless years of only Black & White photography. Someone had lifted the glass off the windshield and you were looking at something *real* and in three dimensions.'

Some audience members were less than complimentary about the new 48-frames-per-second style, though. Peter Sciretta from Slashfilm thought it 'looked like a made-for-television BBC movie. The movement of the actors looked strange, almost as if the performances had been partly sped up. But the dialogue matched the movement of the lips, so it wasn't an effect of speed-ramping. It didn't look cinematic.'

Quickbeam didn't hate it, but described it as 'just a matter of taste.' He continued: 'My gut reaction to what I saw was: "Wow, that sure does look different," because like everyone, I've been used to the film-like quality of projected images used throughout my lifetime of going to the theatre.

'Does it look like High-Def video? Yeah, sort of. The image is actually so pristine, crystal clear, and brightly contrasted that I did have a moment of thinking it was like live broadcast HDTV. But it hasn't been colour-corrected yet, and many nuances of shade and light will be adjusted before 14 December 2012.'

After negative reviews were published both online and offline, Peter Jackson decided to speak out and respond to the complaints as best he could. He told Entertainment Weekly: 'Nobody is going to stop. This technology is going to keep evolving. At first it's unusual because you've never seen a movie like this before. It's literally a new experience, but you know, that doesn't last the entire experience of the film – not by any stretch, (just) 10 minutes or so.

'That's a different experience than if you see a fast-cutting montage at a technical presentation.'

He was hoping that fans would wait and see what the finished movie was like before judging it for themselves – and if people really didn't like the new format then they could always see it in the usual format, as not every cinema would be showing the 48-frames-per-second version.

Dain Ironfoot

- Name: Dain Ironfoot
- Alias: King under the Mountain, King of Durin's Folk
- Race: Dwarf
- Played by: Billy Connolly
- Character description: Dain is one of the great dwarves of his time and is a noble leader. The son of Nain, his weapon of choice is a red axe.

The actor chosen to play Dain was Billy Connolly. In order to do so, it was reported that he had to wear a fat suit as he is 6' and it was thought that by looking fatter, he would appear shorter than he actually is.

Billy was born in Glasgow, Scotland and had a traumatic childhood. His mother abandoned him when he was three years old, his aunt beat him and he was abused by his father between the ages of ten and fifteen. After leaving school when he was fifteen, he worked as a delivery boy and shipyard welder before moving to London to become a guitar and banjo player in a Scottish folk group called The Humblebums. During their performances his banter with the audience between songs went down a storm and this caused him to consider becoming a stand-up comic.

By the late 1960s he was the first proper 'working-class' comedian and had left The Humblebums to go solo. His career has gone from strength to strength ever since. He currently lives in New York with his second wife, Pamela Stephenson, a former actress and comedian who is now a clinical psychologist. She is best known in the UK for coming third in the eighth series of *Strictly Come Dancing*.

Billy might be best known as a comedian but he has appeared in quite a few movies over the years, from children's movie *Lemony Snicket's A Series of Unfortunate Events* to crime thriller movie, *The Boondock Saints*. He was the last member of *The Hobbit* cast to be chosen. Peter Jackson told the *Hollywood Reporter* in February 2012: 'We could not think of a more fitting actor to play Dain Ironfoot, the staunchest and toughest of dwarves, than Billy Connolly, the Big Yin himself. With Billy stepping into this role, the cast of *The Hobbit* is now complete. We can't wait to see him on the Battlefield!'

Jackson might have been looking forward to seeing Billy in the fight scenes but it was a challenge for the 69-year-old actor because his suit of armour was really heavy. Filming the battle scenes was hard work!

DID YOU KNOW?

Billy was looking forward to filming in New Zealand because he had spent time in the country working on *The Last Samurai*, back in 2003. He loved going fishing on his days off and was looking forward to catching some trout again!

Delays

Martin Freeman was asked whether he was concerned about the '*Hobbit* curse' during a press conference shortly before filming for the movie began in March 2011. He admitted: 'I'm not [worried]. There are some bits of bad luck to do with it, I guess, that are almost comical, I suppose. But we're all very optimistic about it. We're all ready to go, just as soon as 2015 rolls around. We will be there and ready.' When he said 2015, the actors playing the dwarves burst into laughter.

Although Martin was joking, in all seriousness there had been delay after delay and for many years there had been the possibility that *The Hobbit* movies would never be made. Peter Jackson and his wife Fran originally wanted to bring out a *Hobbit* movie back in 1995 and they had pitched it but to no avail. The problem they had was that film producer Saul Zaentz had the full rights to *The Lord of the Rings* and the production rights to *The Hobbit*, but he didn't have the distribution rights to *The Hobbit*; they were owned by United Artists (which was for sale at the time) and their attempt to secure the rights was unsuccessful. Because of this, Peter's producer Harvey Weinstein asked him to temporarily forget about *The Hobbit* and instead get on with writing the scripts for *The Lord of the Rings*.

The Lord of the Rings movies were produced by New Line Cinema and came out in 2001, 2002 and 2003. At the time the distribution rights to *The Hobbit* were owned by MGM and in September 2006 they said they wanted to produce the movie alongside New Line Cinema and Jackson; they also wanted a second movie which would explore what happened between the events of *The Hobbit* and those of *The Lord of the Rings*.

In December 2002, Peter Jackson was asked in an

interview with IGN movies whether New Line were interested in having him do *The Hobbit*. He said: 'Well, *The Hobbit*, I can tell you this: the truth is, I've never ever had a single discussion with New Line about *The Hobbit*, at all, ever. The word "Hobbit" has never been mentioned but I do know that they have the rights to *The Hobbit*.

'What the problem with *The Hobbit* is, as I understand it, is that United Artists owns distribution rights to it. And New Line, as part of *The Lord of the Rings* kind of package, they got some sort of production rights to it but they can't distribute it. I mean, New Line can make it, but they can't distribute it. It's sort of weird.

'I suppose there would have to be some sort of production of *The Hobbit*, but they've never spoken to me about it.'

Asked whether he would like to direct it, Jackson confessed: 'I have other films I want to do, and I sort of would feel weird not doing it, if they decided to make it. But on the other hand, I would love to go and just pay 12 bucks and go see what somebody else has done [he laughs]. It would be kind of loony, but it would be easier on me, yes [he laughs].

'So, I don't know, actually. I really don't know which way. If they ever ask me, I have no idea what I would do – I would just have to figure it out at the time.'

A problem arose in March 2005 when Jackson decided

to launch a lawsuit against New Line for lost revenue with regard to *The Lord of the Rings: The Fellowship of The Ring* merchandise and computer games. This angered New Line bosses a great deal and Peter received a phone call in November 2006, telling him that New Line 'would no longer be requiring our services on *The Hobbit* and the *LOTR* "prequel" '. Jackson revealed all in an email to TheOneRing.net: 'This was a courtesy call to let us know that the studio was now actively looking to hire another filmmaker for both projects.

'We've always assumed that we would be asked to make *The Hobbit* and possibly this second film, back to back, as we did the original movies.

'We assumed that our lawsuit with the studio would come to a natural conclusion and we would then be free to discuss our ideas with the studio, get excited and jump on board.

'This outcome is not what we anticipated or wanted, but neither do we see any positive value in bitterness and rancor. We now have no choice but to let the idea of a film of *The Hobbit* go and move forward with other projects.

'We send our very best wishes to whomever has the privilege of making *The Hobbit* and look forward to seeing the film on the big screen.'

Fans were left devastated and Xoanon from the site wrote: 'This is a big blow to the *LOTR* community. I feel like there has been a death in the family, there are a LOT of questions that will remain unanswered for the time being. Why couldn't New Line come to an agreement with PJ? Is there really a time option on the film rights for New Line? Who will they get to direct? Those are some massive shoes to fill, if you ask me. I hope that whoever they get to direct will not try something "new" with the look and feel of PJ's Middle-earth and what is this *LOTR* "prequel" project?'

In January 2007, co-founder of New Line Bob Shaye declared they would never allow Peter Jackson to direct a movie with them. MGM felt disappointed as they wanted him to be involved but thankfully, Shaye made a dramatic U-turn in August and told the *Los Angeles Times* when asked whether they were in talks with Peter: 'Yes, that's a fair statement. Notwithstanding our personal quarrels, I really respect and admire Peter and would love for him to be creatively involved in some way in *The Hobbit*.'

By the December everything was back on and Jackson was to be executive producer of the two *Hobbit* movies. Guillermo del Toro was to be the director and he signed up in April 2008. It was planned for filming to start in 2009, and the movies to be out in December 2010 and 2011, but this wasn't to be as there were yet more delays.

By February 2008, the Tolkien estate had filed a lawsuit against New Line demanding $150 million in compensation because they felt that Tolkien's original deal for 7.5 per cent of the gross from a movie had not been fulfilled. They also wanted the power to terminate any rights to any other movies, so this involved *The Hobbit*.

MGM then decided to recruit private lenders to provide funding for the movies to be made. In a press conference for his movie *Splice* in May 2010, Guillermo del Toro announced: 'There cannot be any start dates until the MGM situation gets resolved. We have designed all the creatures. We've designed the sets and the wardrobe. We have done animatics and planned very lengthy action sequences. We have scary sequences and funny sequences and we are very, very prepared for when it's finally triggered, but we don't know anything until MGM is solved.'

Del Toro couldn't wait any longer for filming to begin and so he bowed out just two days after the press conference. Tolkien fans were left feeling frustrated over the delay, which led to Guillermo explaining to them the reasons why in an interview with 24 Frames at Comic-Con. He said: 'People kept misconstruing that it was MGM. It came from many factors, it wasn't just MGM. These are very complicated movies, economically and politically. You have to get the blessing from three studios.'

Fans were delighted when Peter was named the new director in June 2010 because they felt that finally, filming would start. There was to be another delay, however. The International Federation of Actors decided to issue a 'Do Not Work' order on 24 September 2010. A message on the Screen Actors Guild website stated: 'Members of Canadian Actors Equity, US Actors Equity, the Screen Actors Guild, UK Actors Equity, the American Federation of Television and Radio Artists, the Media, Entertainment & Arts Alliance (Australia) and the Alliance of Canadian Cinema, Television and Radio Artists are advised not to accept work on this non-union production. If you are contacted to be engaged on *The Hobbit* please notify your union immediately.'

If actors ignored the 'Do Not Work' order, they risked being dismissed from their union. This caused all sorts of problems and for a while it looked as though the movies would be filmed in Eastern Europe instead of New Zealand. To try and prevent this happening, thousands of New Zealand residents (including crew members from *The Lord of the Rings* movies) attended protest rallies, not wanting to miss out on the estimated $1.5 billion that the films would generate. In his first interview regarding the 'Do Not Work' order, Peter Jackson told TV ONE's Close Up: 'It's so easy to be caught up in the rhetoric and the big industrial giant versus the small person. It's an emotive thing and very easy to get caught up in that.

'Up until a month ago, no one had even thought in a

million years that this movie was going to leave the country. And then this blacklist was bought on, and the studio said what the hell is going on? and we tried to figure out what the hell was going on.

'At that point, confidence in our country as a stable base to make movies started to erode.'

In October 2010, representatives from the New Zealand government and from Brothers sat down for discussions over two days and the decision was made that the movies would after all be filmed in New Zealand. The government vowed to broaden the financial support they gave to blockbusters and to bring in new legislation, which would hopefully prevent a similar occurrence.

The initial budget for the movies was $500,000,000 and filming was due to begin in February 2011. There was one last delay due to Peter needing an urgent operation for a perforated ulcer but filming finally started on 28 March.

Design

Weta Workshop is a special effects company specialising in creating props for movies and TV series. It was founded by Richard Taylor and Tania Rodgers in 1987 and Weta Digital, the digital arm, was formed in 1993. Weta Workshop made the sets, weapons, costumes, armour and creatures for *The Lord of the Rings* movies and was tasked with doing the same for *The Hobbit*. Their senior prosthetics supervisor and visual creature effects art director Gino Acevedo had a big part to play in the props and make-up for *The Hobbit* movies.

The concept artists on the movies were John Howe and Alan Lee. They were the chief conceptual designers for *The Lord of the Rings* and are Middle-earth experts. When Guillermo del Toro was the director, he hired the comic book artists Mike Mignola and Wayne Barlowe to help with some of the designs. Guillermo explained what he was trying to do in an online chat with fans. He said: 'I plan to mix CGI [computer generated imagery] and physical in such a way that your eye wonders which is which – keep your mind busy but never allowing for the weaknesses of either tool to take over. Yes, I have, by trial and error, learned that both tools need to be mixed and how much they must be mixed to succeed in creating environments and living creatures. Weta is the lead house, absolutely, but we will expand the creature team and beef up the prosthetics team. Imagine a physical creature with a radio controlled muscle/facial system but with partial CGI replacement on the head or mouth, etc. and you'll start to get the idea.'

Del Toro also discussed what fans should expect from the designs in *The Hobbit*. He said: 'The basic designs, the pre-established designs will be only "updated" in so far as the epoch difference. Half a century more or less, which in Middle-earth terms is not that much but think about how much our world has changed from, say, 2001 to now. The new settings and designs should blend in enough not to feel like a completely different world but yes, the movies are bound to have some distinctive stylistic imprint.'

He wanted each dwarf to have an individual look but still look like the others in some way, as he explained during a chat with Indalo Productions. He said: 'The book demands that you make them believable, and that you make at least the name of the thirteen dwarves, the ones that will have fully speaking parts as memorable, but officially you have a story of all of them, and not treat them as secondary characters. The idea is you're watching *The Magnificent Seven* in the middle of the movie – they were recruited for a reason. So if all thirteen look kind of alike, and all thirteen – or worse even, if they all look too much unlike each other, you know, so you can almost differentiate them with tag, then that's almost worse. So you have to strike a real balance so that when that group comes in those are the "Seven Samurai" and you know by the way they interact with each other that he was chosen because he keeps vigil, he's in command, this one is loyal, these two are fighting all the time but they're willing to die for each other, blah, blah, blah – you have to make all that, all on the run. Everything is a challenge.'

He confessed to DigitalActing.com that designing *The Hobbit* took a long time: 'It took almost a year, which for me is very, very long because normally I take about a third of that time to design movies like *Hellboy*. And if you actually take into account we have three or four times the number of artists [chuckles]. We produced hundreds, literally hundreds, of drawings; dozens and dozens of maquettes; dozens of material tests. It's epic. And we are still going to be designing into production.'

In *The Lord of the Rings* movies, the trolls, eagles and other animals didn't speak, but in *The Hobbit* books Tolkien has the trolls, eagles and Smaug the dragon talking, so fans wondered whether they would speak in the movies. When asked in a fan chat how much the portrayal of these creatures would change in *The Hobbit*, Guillermo replied: 'I think it should be done exactly as in the book – the "talking beast" motif has to exist already to allow for that great character that is Smaug. It is far more jarring to have a linear movie and then – out of the blue – a talking Dragon.'

He added: 'One of the main mistakes with talking dragons is to shape the mouth like a snub Simian one in order to achieve a dubious lip-synch – a point which eluded me, particularly in *Eragon*, since their link is a psychic one.

'To me, Smaug is the perfect example of a great creature defined by its look and design, yes, but also, very importantly, by his movement and one little hint – its environment – think about it the way he is scaled, moves and is lit, limited or enhanced by his location, weather conditions, light conditions, time of the year, etc. That's all I can say without spoilers.'

DID YOU KNOW?

Guillermo's all-time favourite movie dragons are Vermithrax Pejorative from *Dragonslayer* and Maleficent from the Disney classic, *Sleeping Beauty*.

Dori

- Name: Dori
- Alias: None
- Race: Dwarf of the House of Durin
- Played by: Mark Hadlow
- Character description: Dori is a dwarf who wears a purple hood. He is the eldest of three brothers, with Nori his middle brother and Ori the youngest. Dori looks out for Ori and despite quarrelling with his brothers from time to time, he would die for them. He is a keen flute player and is the strongest dwarf on the quest with Bilbo.

The actor chosen to play Dori was Mark Hadlow. A New Zealand actor and comedian, he always loved performing at school but never really considered becoming an actor because he didn't think you could earn enough money from it. Mark joined the Navy for three years, joining their band as a cornet player, but then decided to give acting a go. He wanted to be the centre of attention and loved making people laugh, something he couldn't do playing an instrument!

Mark is best known for playing Harry in the 2005 movie *King Kong*, and another character called Harry in the New Zealand TV sitcom *Willy Nilly*. In the show he played one of two brothers who have lived a sheltered life on a farm, caring for their mother until her death. As well as acting in movies and TV shows, Mark loves the theatre and has been directing and producing many plays at Christchurch's Court Theatre.

When he started filming *The Hobbit*, Mark struggled to remember the names of all the dwarves but eventually he got to know them all, and the names of the actors who played them. The other actors find it funny that Mark likes to wear Naval uniforms for interviews. James Nesbitt who plays Bofur is the joker of the cast and in a production video discussed the other dwarf actors. He said: 'Some of them actually look pretty bad before they get into the prosthetics. In fact, for some of them, the prosthetic is making them look better, to tell you the truth. Er, which says something; er, Mark Hadlow, for example, springs to mind.'

Mark and his fellow dwarves recorded a hilarious 'first look at the dwarves' section for the Rise Up Christchurch Telethon, which was held three months after the Christchurch earthquake to help raise money to rebuild the city. In the 12-hour telethon, over $1 million was donated. In their exclusive backstage video, Mark and his fellow actors were all dressed up as garden gnomes, with colourful hats, white beards and rosy cheeks. They joked it had taken three hours to have their make-up applied and that the bells on their hats would look amazing in 3D. Richard Armitage had knelt down and put shoes on his knees so he was completely ready, while the characters supposed to be wearing fat suits had cushions shoved up their tops. It was a hilarious video and all done to try and get as many people as possible to donate to the Christchurch appeal.

Drogo Baggins
- Name: Drogo
- Alias: None
- Race: Hobbit
- Played by: Originally Ryan Gage

• Character description: Drogo is the father of Frodo.
  He drowned while out fishing with his wife Primula,
  leaving Frodo an orphan.

The actor Ryan Gage was initially chosen to play Drogo
but he was promoted to the much bigger part of Alfrid.
Director Peter Jackson did not reveal the name of the
new actor to play Drogo and so, prior to the release of
the first movie, fans were thinking Ryan would be
playing Drogo, too.

Dwalin

• Name: Dwalin
• Alias: None
• Race: Dwarf of the House of Durin
• Played by: Graham McTavish
• Character description: Dwalin is the brother of Balin.
  A great fighter, he has a blue beard and wears a golden
  belt and a dark-green hood.

The actor chosen to play Dwalin was Graham McTavish,
a British actor who is best known for playing
Commander Lewis in the movie *Rambo* (2008). Over the
years, he has appeared in several top British dramas, from
Red Dwarf to *The Bill*, *Taggart* to *Casualty*. In the USA he

has appeared as Desmond's drill sergeant in *Lost,* Ferguson in *Prison Break* and Mikhail Novakovich in *24.*

DID YOU KNOW?

Graham McTavish provided the voice of Decepticon Thundercracker in the video game *Transformers: War for Cybertron.*

Graham hadn't read *The Hobbit* until he found out about the movies but he had read all three of the *Lord of The Rings* books when he was eighteen. When he talked to his male friends and acquaintances about the books, the vast majority said they preferred *The Hobbit* and for many it had been the first book they'd read as teenagers. He hopes fans of the book won't mind that the actors and director Peter Jackson changed a few things as they brought the characters from the book to life.

For his first audition Graham had had to read for the part of Thorin. (He found out later that a lot of his fellow cast members had had to read the same.) The first audition went well and the casting director asked him to come back again for another audition. For his second audition he read for the part of Dwalin, alongside a fantastic reader who read the other characters' lines in the scene. Graham feels he owes the reader that day a lot because he was able to just get on with acting as best he could because the reader was so good. After he'd completed one read-through the casting director was going to let him go, but Graham felt he could do it a bit better and so he convinced the casting director to let him have one more go. Once he'd finished, Graham had a long and anxious wait over many weeks to find out if he'd done enough. Eventually he got another call back with Philippa Boyens and Fran Walsh, who co-wrote the script with Peter Jackson.

Graham was excited and nervous during the call back because he was so close to securing the part. Peter Jackson had planned on being there, but he was feeling unwell because of his stomach ulcer so was in an adjoining room. Graham chatted about the part to Philippa and Fran, then did more read-throughs with the same reader as before. After they'd left the room, he had a chat with the reader, who confessed that he thought Graham would get the part. He was right!

Once Graham found out that he would be playing Dwalin, he told his wife Gwen, who was thrilled because she (like Billy Connolly's wife, Pamela Stephenson) is originally from New Zealand, so she would be going home. He then got himself a personal trainer so he could improve his levels of fitness – he had to be physically prepared for the fight scenes to make sure he didn't injure himself once filming started. There were five months to get ready, and that involved lots of gym sessions and a change to his diet.

DID YOU KNOW?

Graham's favourite *Lord of the Rings* character is Aragorn/Strider.

Graham and Gwen love parties and decided to throw a house-warming party in their Wellington house shortly before filming began. It was a great way of getting to know people on a personal level. Scriptwriter Philippa Boyens had the same idea and so there ended up being two parties in two nights. The dwarves' actors and their families thoroughly enjoyed themselves but it was tricky for them all trying to remember each other's names. Ian McKellen (who plays Gandalf) cheated a bit because his agent had sent him a book with photos of everyone with their names and their character's name; he'd also done his own research by googling each actor.

Elrond

- Name: Elrond
- Alias: Lord of Rivendell, Lord Elrond, Master Elrond
- Race: Half-elven
- Played by: Hugo Weaving
- Character description: Elrond is an elf friend, with grey eyes and dark hair. He is wise and a great warrior. His house is the perfect haven for anyone who happens to stay there.

The actor chosen to play Elrond in *The Lord of the Rings* and *The Hobbit* movies was Hugo Weaving. Born in

Austin, Nigeria, he spent his childhood in Nigeria, Australia and the UK. He attended Queen Elizabeth's Hospital School in Bristol for three years for his O-levels but then moved permanently to Australia. Hugo studied at Knox Grammar School, Sydney before attending the National Institute of Dramatic Art.

DID YOU KNOW?

Geoffrey Rush, Mel Gibson and Cate Blanchett also studied at the National Institute of Dramatic Art.

Since graduating, Hugo has most enjoyed appearing on the stage but he has also had a successful TV and movie career. In 1991 he won an Australian Film Institute Award for playing Martin in *Proof* and in 1998, he picked up another one for playing Eddie Rodney Fleming in *The Interview*. He has won 13 other top acting awards.

Hugo is best known for playing Elrond, Red Skull in *Captain America: The First Avenger* and Agent Smith in *The Matrix*. He also provides the voice for Megatron in the *Transformers* movies. In a 2000 interview with the *Daily Telegraph* during filming, he said: '*Lord of the Rings* compared to *Matrix*, it doesn't compare. It's huge. *The Matrix* was huge but it was kind of manageable – I just think it's kind of madness to do three films at once, really.

I think they know that now, but they can't stop. But they are doing a fantastic job.'

Before he was officially signed up for *The Hobbit* movies Hugo talked to HitFix journalist Drew McWeeny in 2010 about whether he would want to be in the movies. He said: 'I'd be interested in doing it. I would love to work with Guillermo del Toro very much. I think he's a fantastic talent, a great director.'

Asked whether he thought *The Hobbit* movies would pose any fresh challenges because he is so familiar with the role, he replied: 'Absolutely, and I would be interested in revisiting that in a way because the book is tonally quite different from *Lord of the Rings*. I think there's a slightly more innocent quality to it and it's a slightly different world. It's the same physical world but the writer was at a different age when he wrote it, and he wrote it in a different spirit. So you might be using some of the same actors and the same team but you might want to have a slightly different take on it and I think that would be pretty interesting.'

DID YOU KNOW?

Hugo Weaving is the uncle of Samara Weaving, who plays Indigo Walker in the Australian soap *Home and Away*.

Back in May 2011, Ian McKellen confirmed Hugh's casting on his blog. He explained that they were filming the scenes in the movie without Bilbo and that Hugh was back to play Elrond. He mentioned that Hugh had recently been acting in the Chekov play *Uncle Vanya* alongside Cate Blanchett (Galadriel).

FILM FACT:

On Day 38 of shooting they filmed the scenes at Rivendell. Richard Armitage (Thorin) enjoyed meeting Elrond (Hugo) so much, telling the backstage cameras: 'Dining at his table makes you think you're stepping into Middle-earth.'

Fans

Eric Vespe is a movie critic and one of the biggest fans of *The Hobbit*. He was invited to be an extra in Hobbiton while writing behind-the-scenes reports for *AintItCool.com* and had an absolute blast. There were 60 adult hobbits and 10 child hobbits involved in the market scene and he was chosen to sell Bilbo a fish. Eric had been approached by Peter, who had asked him, 'How do you feel about fish?'

Eric told him he didn't have any fish phobias and was up for it, so he was given the part of a fishmonger. He had to sell a fish to Bilbo. The extra who had originally been given the role was moved to another part of the market, and Eric was instructed to stand behind a counter, surrounded by fake fish and eels.

As they rehearsed, Martin Freeman asked Eric what his hobbit name was but he didn't have one. Peter explained to him that there is a website that takes your real name and then gives you your hobbit name. His assistant got the website up on his iPhone and within a few seconds Eric found out his hobbit name was Fredegar Chubb!

Eric was then given a line to say when he passed over the fish: ''ere you go, sir!' So many *Hobbit* fans would have given anything to have been in his hobbit feet – he was going to be in the biggest movie of 2012!

Superfan Vince Donovan from Pennsylvania, USA didn't get to be an extra but he gets to visit his own piece of Hobbiton every day. Vince first read *The Hobbit* and *The Lord of the Rings* in 1964/65 and started collecting different editions of the books in the 1970s. He then began collecting themed items, figurines, paintings and pipes. Pretty soon the collection was taking over his house.

Vince decided to speak to some architects about an idea he had: he wanted to build a hobbit house. They did rough drawings and plans in 2004 and then the architects did some proper drawings, based on what they read in Tolkien's books. They studied all the pictures available that had been drawn over the years by people imagining what a hobbit–hole would look like. The biggest challenge was getting the round front door because Vince wanted it to be completely round; he didn't want a straight bit for a hinge so had a custom-made hinge created by an ironworker. Once it was finished Vince transferred all of his collection to his hobbit house, and he can now relax in his hobbit home whenever life gets too much.

If you want to find out the latest news on *The Hobbit* movies, then why not visit a fan site or two? TheOneRing.net is the biggest Tolkien fan site on the Internet and they have even created a free App for fans to download onto their phones – just search for *The Hobbit* by Fizzit Apps on iTunes or Google Marketplace.

Arguably the biggest *Hobbit* and *Lord of the Rings* fans are the actors and crewmembers themselves. They have an absolute blast filming the movies and struggle when it's all over. Billy Boyd, who played Pippin in *The Lord of the Rings* movies, really wanted a cameo in *The Hobbit* but he wasn't permitted to do so (he had wanted to play the father of Pippin) but told the *Daily Record*: 'No, I wouldn't think anything will come of that but I am definitely going to go down there – I haven't been back since the premiere of *Return Of The King*.

'Most of the guys have been back for a little trip or something but I have not managed it. I have been talking to Dom and Elijah and we are all going to go back this year. We will all go together, like a reunion trip. We want to go and see the sets.

'And while we're there, there must be something for us. They must need a Hobbit in the background somewhere. I can even put the big feet on myself!'

Fili

- Name: Fili
- Alias: None
- Race: Dwarf of the House of Durin
- Played by: Dean O'Gorman
- Character description: Fili is a young dwarf with a yellow beard, silver belt and blue hood. He plays the fiddle and has the best eyesight out of the 13 dwarves who go on the quest. Fili is the brother of Kili and they are the nephews of Thorin.

The actor initially chosen to play Fili was former *EastEnders* star Rob Kazinsky, but owing to personal reasons, he had to pull out in April 2011. Director Peter Jackson left the following message on his Facebook page: 'I am sad to report that Rob Kazinsky, who was cast in the role of Fili, is having to leave *The Hobbit* and return home, for personal reasons. Rob has been terrific to work with and his enthusiasm and infectious sense of humour will be missed by all of us. I should say that Rob's departure will not affect ongoing filming of *The Hobbit*, nor will it impact on work done to date, as we had yet to film much of Fili's storyline. At the moment we are shooting scenes featuring Bilbo without the dwarves, which will give us time to find a new Fili. I'll keep everyone posted with updates as they come.'

Rob also tweeted a message to his followers shortly afterwards: 'Thanks for all your support. Peter and team have been the most wonderful and supportive team to work for and it's with a truly sad heart that things have turned out this way. *The Hobbit* will go on to be as great as I've seen and I will miss the family and friends that I've here, from every disaster I've tried to make an opportunity.'

Rob must have been extremely disappointed because he was so enthusiastic about appearing in *The Hobbit* movies. Out of all the dwarf actors at the first press conference he had been the one who answered the most questions.

In May 2011, Peter Jackson updated fans and announced on his Facebook page that Dean O'Gorman would be replacing Rob: 'I'm very pleased to be welcoming two new cast members to our team.

'Dean O'Gorman will be playing Fili. Dean's a terrific Kiwi actor, who I am thrilled to be working with. He's recently been in an excellent TV series down here called *The Almighty Johnsons*, and I should let fans of that show know that our shooting schedule allows Dean to continue with a second series next year. Dean will be joining us next week.

'It's been a great week, and I'm looking forward to the next few. It's going to be interesting…'

Dean was a great choice to play Fili as he is a very experienced actor, having been in the business since he was a child. He was born in Auckland, New Zealand and his first role was playing Tony Garrett in the 1990 TV movie *The Rogue Stallion* but he is best known for playing Iolaus in *Young Hercules* and Homa in *Xena: Warrior Princess*. Many people think Dean chooses fantasy roles on purpose but he insists this isn't the case, telling *Geek Syndicate*: 'I think it's coincidence. I wouldn't say I consciously choose fantasy stuff but it does seem to be popping up lately.'

He also talked about his favourite fantasy TV shows and movies when growing up: 'As a kid I loved *Star Wars* (I even still have the old cardboard Death Star), but that's not really fantasy, is it? *Krull*, I remember seeing that with Dad and loving it, but they never made toys of that film. I was into things like MASK (where illusion is the ultimate weapon) and GI Joe.'

DID YOU KNOW?

By the time he was ten, Dean O'Gorman was a karate black belt.

In his spare time, Dean is a keen painter and photographer and recently recreated some scenes from the Vietnam War to photograph. He gets his artistic streak from his dad, who is a landscape painter. When he was twelve, he got his first acting job in the TV movie *Raider of the South Seas*. He did more acting work, but got into photography at college and since then he's done both successfully, often taking headshot photos of his actor friends.

Dean's showreel was put together by Gareth Williams, so if you want to watch it, head over to www.garethwilliamsshowreels.com.

Filming

The movies were split into three blocks so the cast and crew could have breaks to recover, reflect and prepare for the next session. Block one was shot on the K-Stage, Stone Street Studios, Wellington. Block two was on location and block three was back in the studio. They had 254 days of shooting in total, so after 50 days, director Peter Jackson gave the members of the crew a T-shirt each with 254 days crossed out and 200 to go. This made everyone feel even more tired!

Although an extremely long shoot, it went fast for the cast and crew. Richard Armitage (who plays Thorin) told MTV in January 2012: 'It's really weird because when we started it was just this enormous mountain to climb, but actually, it's going so fast. I think we've gotten to the halfway point now. It's been really intense, but so exciting. We literally just finished our location shoot that we've been out on the road, seeing most of New Zealand. It's been the best thing I've ever worked on in my life, by far!'

The 7th production video blog was filmed at Stone Street Studios. It used to be an old paint factory and Peter explained: 'We got hold of it just before we started *Lord of the Rings*. We built one sound studio (Stage A) for *Lord of the Rings*, we built another one on *King Kong* (Stage K), and we built a couple more here for *The Hobbit* (G and F Stages). It's actually a great place to make movies right now.'

DID YOU KNOW?

The K Stage was named the K-Stage even though they hadn't got up to that letter in the alphabet because 'K' stands for King Kong!

On the first day of filming the cast and crew were treated to a Powhiri Welcoming Ceremony. After the Powhiri people had performed a haka (a traditional war cry/dance) to welcome the cast and crew, Richard Armitage represented the cast, saying in Maori: 'For those who have passed into the veil of darkness. Travel safe, travel safe, travel safe.' He then spoke in English: 'My name is Richard. I'm from London, England. [Everyone started clapping.] I would like to give thanks on behalf of everyone here to visitors for this ceremony, for this celebration, for the blessing of the sound stage and for the welcome you have offered to us. We are all deeply honoured to be here. And to everyone that has waited so long for this day, to begin this extraordinary journey filming *The Hobbit*, I would like to wish them good luck, good health and good harmony.'

Martin Freeman then had something to share. He said: 'My name's Martin Freeman, I'm in the cast as well. He started with everything I was going to say in Maori. It has been a long time coming today, even longer than we thought it would be, so thank you everybody, very much.'

In the first break Peter Hambleton (Glóin) went on holiday to the South Island of New Zealand with his wife, while William Kircher (Bifur) did some decorating at his house and Ian McKellen went back to London because he was playing Don Antonio in the Eduardo De Filippo play, *The Syndicate*. James Nesbitt flew to Pebble Beach, California to play golf and then went to see his family in Ireland. Jed Brophy joked that he was going to get a tan to 'freak out' the make-up artists; Richard Armitage was just planning a four-week break, the crew were playing lie-ins. Mark Hadlow (Dori) was going to Australia with his wife to see his eldest daughter, then planning lots of golf and swimming. Conan Stevens

(Azog) was looking forward to going home to Thailand and catching up with his mates. Sylvester McCoy (Radagast) was going to Barcelona to meet *Doctor Who* fans from Spain because he played the seventh Doctor Who in the years 1987–89, as well as appearing in a charity special in 1993 and in a TV movie in 1996. Andy Serkis planned to see his family and maybe go on holiday. Peter Jackson didn't really get a break as he was on location scouting, then in the cutting room on the first Monday; also talking to the designers about arrangements for the second block, then involved in discussions about what sets needed to be built for the second block, plus preproduction starts, as well as editing block one, so not much time off at all.

DID YOU KNOW?

Peter Jackson admits that had there been 3D technology in the days when he was shooting *The Lord of the Rings*, he would have liked to take advantage of it. He did, however, take photos of the cast with a 3D camera, in case the material could be used in the future, and hopes they'll be included on a Blu-ray in the future.

While filming *The Hobbit*, the crew got to see the scenes in 3D as they created them, which was really exciting.

Peter discussed how he likes to work with News.com.au. He said: 'I tell you what I always try and do – I try to think of how I can do things better. I always show up on set in the morning and I'm constantly thinking, "OK, this is what we need to do, let's set it up. Let's look at the camera angle, let's rehearse; now, how do I improve this?"

'To me, there's never anything that's perfect. Anything you do or imagine can always be made better. So if an actor does a take and it looks good, before I move on to the next shot I'm going to think to myself, "Is there anything I can think of how we could improve it and do one more take?" Whether it's a camera move or a note I give to the actor or the way the lights are – anything at all, so I try to always keep that process in my head, saying, "Don't settle for anything, always push, push, push." Which makes for an interesting day. It makes for a tiring day, but it certainly keeps me on my toes.'

When filming, they used 48 Red Epic cameras on 17 3D rigs. Peter decided to name them all and in a production video, he revealed there was one called Walter (the name of his granddad), another was Ronald (his uncle's name), one called Emily (Fran's grandma's name), one called Perkins (Fran's dog's name), another was Bill (Peter's dad's name), one called Fergus (their pug's name), plus Tricky Woo (their Pekinese dog's name), one called Stan (another one of their pug's names) and many more. In an interview with Collider.com. Orlando Bloom (who plays Legolas) revealed what using RED Epics is like, and what it's like to film a 3D movie. He said: [*Musketeers* – another 3D movie he has done] was shot in 3D, as is *The Hobbit*, as you said with the RED Epics. Those are small cameras, those RED Epics. I mean they're doing steadicam, they're doing over-the-shoulder, they're doing everything with those cameras, and it's 3D, which is to me pretty phenomenal. My experience of it is that it's the same – I mean, it seems to be becoming the norm, which is crazy in many regards but I guess as time goes on things move on forward.

'The cameras are probably getting lighter and smaller, as they are with the RED Epics but they're doing remarkable things on *The Hobbit* with these cameras that I couldn't have imagined, and [*Musketeers*] was shot with James Cameron's cameras, the ARRI Alexa. There was a little bit more set-up time and stuff I would say, but not massively so. The shoots are still the same sort of length and as an actor your experience is not any different, you're still relating to other actors in the same way. I think as an audience member you get quality when it's shot in 3D.'

On Tuesday, 12 April 2011, Peter filled in the fans on what was happening. He wrote on his Facebook page: 'I thought I'd address the news that has been reported about us shooting THE HOBBIT at 48 frames per second, and explain to you what my thoughts are about this…

'It looks much more lifelike, and it is much easier to watch, especially in 3-D. We've been watching HOBBIT tests and dailies at 48 fps now for several months, and we often sit through two hours worth of footage without getting any eye strain from the 3-D. It looks great, and we've actually become used to it now, to the point that other film experiences look a little primitive.'

Frodo Baggins

- Name: Frodo Baggins
- Alias: The Ringbearer
- Race: Hobbit
- Played by: Elijah Wood
- Character description: Frodo was adopted by his cousin Bilbo Baggins after his parents died. A medium-sized hobbit, he has brown, curly hair. He shares his birthday (22 September) with Bilbo.

The actor chosen to play Frodo was Elijah Wood. He had already played Frodo in *The Lord of the Rings* trilogy. Frodo does not appear in the book version of *The Hobbit*, but director Peter Jackson and the other scriptwriters made the decision to give him a small part in *The Hobbit* movies.

Elijah is an American actor from Cedar Rapids, Iowa. A born entertainer, he secured his first acting jobs as a young child. He started out acting in TV adverts and had bit parts in TV shows before landing the part of Michael Kaye in the 1990 movie *Avalon*, which was his first big break. Elijah has appeared in movies alongside Mel Gibson, Macaulay Culkin, Ron Perlman, Kevin Costner and Sigourney Weaver, to name but a few, and proved to everyone that he was a talented adult actor, not just a has-been child actor. Eager to do something out of the ordinary to get the part of Frodo, he asked his director friend George Huang to help him film an audition tape. Elijah dressed in his best hobbit outfit and then the two of them went into the Californian woods to film a few scenes. Afterwards they edited it together and then Elijah sent the footage off to the casting agent, hoping he'd done enough.

Since filming the last *The Lord of the Rings* movie, he has played Patrick in *Eternal Sunshine of the Spotless Mind*, Kevin in *Sin City*, Mumble (*Happy Feet*) and Ryan Newman in the TV series *Wilfred*. He also set up his own music label – Simian Records. Elijah always tells people that actually he's a nerd and regrets he can no longer attend events such as Comic-Con (comic book convention) and walk the floor because fans swamp him. He told Collider.com: 'It's weird – in my daily life, I can go anywhere without a problem, but that's such a concentrated amalgam of those folks that it's difficult. We're part of that, too – it's not a me-versus-them – but it's really hard 'cause I want to. I've been there so many times, and I did walk the floor the first time I went. We were there to promote *Rings* before it came out, and I did walk the floor and it was radical. I checked out all the toy booths. It was awesome, meeting artists. But after the first movie came out, it was pretty apparent that I couldn't do that again. And I've thought about getting a costume or a mask and walking around that way, but it's a little difficult. A bunch of people do that – I think Simon Pegg does that. I've definitely thought about doing that.'

To date, his biggest acting role has been Frodo and so he was over the moon when asked if he would like to star in *The Hobbit* movies. Elijah told the *Salt Lake Tribune*: 'I was there for a month. It didn't actually take that much time for the work – it was sort of half vacation and catching up with old friends and half work.

'I stood on the hill, looking at *The Hobbit* holes and I was, like, "I turned 19 here and I'm 30 now." It was such a weird thing. And a lot of the same crew were there. That was the most bizarre – it felt like taking a step back in time almost. It was extraordinary.'

On the set of Hobbiton, he divulged to the Production Video 5: 'I'll never forget that feeling of coming to Hobbiton for the first time – so much time spent in this universe with these characters. I don't know, there's so many feelings of nostalgia and history.'

DID YOU KNOW?

Elijah Wood is a massive *True Blood*, *The Wire* and *Mad Men* fan. For a while he liked tuning in to *Biggest Loser*!

Because Elijah has only a small part he was looking forward to seeing the movies in the cinema as a Tolkien fan, rather than as an actor. He hadn't seen that much of it being filmed so he would be seeing things with fresh eyes. In the beginning, he did receive some negative responses from fans because they didn't think he should have appeared at all since his character hadn't even been born by *The Hobbit*'s conclusion, but he managed to set their minds at rest in a few interviews he did. He explained that it was all done cleverly and in an appropriate way that adds something to the story, not just for the sake of it.

Elijah loves playing Frodo so much, and still has *The Hobbit* feet that director Peter Jackson gifted him when they finished filming the third *The Lord of the Rings* movie. He reminisced to the *Radio Times*: 'They're in a box on a shelf somewhere. They're made of latex and I haven't actually checked on them in quite some time. They may have rotted by now – I should probably go and see.'

He was also given the ring, which he keeps in a box, too. For a while he used to wear it, but he doesn't now because so much time has passed since he filmed *The Lord of the Rings* movies, but he might be tempted to slip it on again, one day.

Galadriel

- Name: Galadriel
- Alias: The Lady of Lórien, Lady of Light, Storm Queen, The Lady of the Galadhrim, White Lady, Queen Galadriel, Sorceress of the Golden Wood, Elf-Witch, The Lady of the Wood
- Race: Noldorin Elf
- Played by: Cate Blanchett
- Character description: Galadriel does not appear in *The Hobbit* book, but Peter Jackson decided to include her in back-story scenes of *The Hobbit* movies. A tall elf with ageless beauty, she has long, shining golden hair, shot with silver.

Australian actress Cate Blanchett had previously played Galadriel in *The Lord of the Rings* movies and was chosen to play the same part in *The Hobbit* films. Highly talented, she has picked up many big awards throughout her career, including an Oscar, two BAFTAs and two Golden Globes. When Blanchett signed up for *The Hobbit* movies, Peter Jackson released a statement to the press. In it, he stated: 'Cate is one of my favorite actors to work with and I couldn't be more thrilled to have her reprise the role she so beautifully brought to life in the earlier films.'

Cate was also very excited and during an interview for her movie *Hanna* (2011), she told Collider.com: 'Obviously, Galadriel is only a small part of *The Lord of the Rings* trilogy but it was the greatest three weeks I think I've ever spent. Peter Jackson and Fran, his partner-in-crime, are two of the great gifts to the film industry, I think – certainly one of the greatest gifts to New Zealand. I haven't seen a script yet, so I don't know what I'll be doing. Obviously Galadriel doesn't factor very strongly in *The Hobbit*.'

They hadn't told her when she would be filming, only that it would be in 'the middle of the year'. She must have really trusted Peter and Fran to sign up without seeing a script because she didn't know what she was letting herself in for. But Cate wasn't the only person in her household to be excited; her kids were excited, too. She revealed to *German Interview* magazine: 'They thought it was crazy exciting. My two older ones have seen *The Lord of the Rings* trilogy. Since I have kids, I am doing a lot fewer movies than I have before, but my three sons have grown up with trailers and being on sets. Nevertheless, this story is something special.'

Cate Blanchett is one of Australia's best-loved actresses. She was born in Melbourne, Victoria, and started acting at school but had no great ambition to become an actress. After finishing college, she went travelling and found herself working as an actress in an Arabic boxing movie when she was short of cash in Egypt. When she realised how actors, through their acting, have the power to move people she decided she wanted to be a full-time actress.

Blanchett studied at the National Institute of Dramatic Art in Kensington, Australia and graduated in 1992. She began appearing in plays in Australia, firstly Caryl Churchill's *Top Girls* and then Tim Daly's *Kafka Dances*. Theatre-goers and critics were impressed with her performances and she was given the 1993 Sydney Theatre Critics Circle Newcomer Award. She continued with her stage career, winning more awards, before starring in the hit Australian TV drama *Heartland*. Cate's first movie was *Paradise Road*, which also starred Glenn Close and came out in 1997. Her big break came a year later, playing the lead in the 1998 movie, *Elizabeth*. It brought her international fame. She is best known for this role and for playing Galadriel. As well as appearing in blockbusters such as *Indiana Jones and the Kingdom of the Crystal Skull* and *The Aviator*, Cate spends a lot of her time on stage. She is an artistic director of Sydney Theatre Company, alongside her husband Andrew Upton. Andrew is a playwright, screenwriter and director and together they have their own film production company, Dirty Films.

DID YOU KNOW?

Cate and her husband got engaged after just three weeks of dating.

Being in *The Lord of the Rings* movies opened a new world of acting for Blanchett. She hadn't really worked with prosthetics and blue screens before and so to begin with, it felt a bit strange. As she explained to Total Film: 'I wanted to work with Peter Jackson. The role was oddly secondary and the consequence of playing it was beside the point.'

In an interview with Fox Television Network, she admitted that she had always wanted to be in a movie where she had to wear pointed ears. After she finished shooting her scenes for *The Lord of the Rings*, she was given bronze castings of her ears as a gift.

Despite her fame, Cate has remained down-to-earth and the exact opposite of a diva. Total Film asked her how she likes to be treated on set and she replied: 'With respect. All I want is respect. Everyone wants to be respected, don't they? You want your work to be respected, whether you're working in the props department, whether you're the cinematographer, the make-up person or whatever. You want to feel your effort is being appreciated. I haven't got every ounce of my being invested in film; I can contextualise because I've had children and worked in the theatre. I come from a different angle to someone who started off as a child actor or who crossed over from being a musician or a model.'

Galion
- Name: Galion
- Alias: King's Butler, Old Galion
- Race: Elf of the Woodland Realm
- Played by: Unconfirmed
- Character description: Galion is a golden-haired elf and fond of wine. When he drinks too much, he falls asleep and is grumpy when woken up.

Gandalf
- Name: Gandalf
- Alias: Gandalf the Grey, Gandalf the White,

Mithrandir, Olórin, Stormcrow, Greyhame, Grey Fool,
The White Rider, Incánus, Tharkûn, LáthSpell, Grey
Pilgrim, Grey Wanderer
- Race: Maiar/Istari/Ithryn
- Played by: Sir Ian McKellen
- Character description: Gandalf is a wizard with a
  white beard, a pointed blue hat, a grey cloak, a silver
  scarf and black boots.

Lots of actors have played Gandalf over the years. In the
1978 animated *The Lord of the Rings*, he was voiced by
William Squire; in the 1977 and 1979 animated *The
Hobbit* and *The Return of the King* he was voiced by
Michael Hordern and in the 1981 and 1955 BBC radio
adaptations, he was voiced by Norman Shelley. For the
2001–03 *The Lord of the Rings* movies Sir Ian McKellen
was cast as Gandalf and he was one of the first actors
signed up for *The Hobbit* movies.

Sir Ian McKellen is originally from Burnley, England
but he grew up in Wigan, Lancashire. One of his earliest
memories is going to see *Peter Pan* at the Manchester
Opera House when he was three years old. His family
loved the theatre and his sister Jean took him to see his
first Shakespeare play – *Twelfth Night* – at Wigan's Little
Theatre. Every week, they would go to see a play at
Bolton's Hippodrome as well as any ballet or operas

showing in the local area. Ian was a keen actor at school and he joined the Hopefield Miniature Theatre.

He told IGN FilmForce: 'I went to study English at Cambridge, and there did a great deal of acting with friends who were determined to become professionals: Trevor Nunn – who now runs the National Theatre, Sir Derek Jacobi, Sir David Frost, Peter Cook, and others. I caught the bug there. It was then that I realised, "Well, if they're going to be able to do it in the professional theatre, then perhaps I can myself." When I left Cambridge, I applied to regional repertory theatres in the UK and got accepted by one of them. And here I am, still at it.'

In his early career he was in several Shakespeare plays, playing Shallow in *Henry IV*, Iago in *Othello* and Macbeth in the play of the same name. In 2007, he joined the Royal Shakespeare Company for productions of *King Lear* and *The Seagull*; they were a sell-out. Two years later, he wowed theatre audiences again in *Waiting for Godot* with Patrick Stewart.

Sir Ian's first movie role was back in 1969 when he played George Matthews in *A Touch of Love*. He began appearing in TV series and movies for television before he became better known as a movie actor in the 1990s; he was nominated for an Oscar for his performance as James Whale in the 1998 movie *God and Monsters*. Today, he is best known for playing Magneto in the *X-Men* movies and Gandalf in *The Lord of the Rings*.

After Sir Ian agreed to once more play Gandalf in *The Hobbit* movies, he had to rearrange his schedule because there was no firm start date for filming because of the delays. Originally, he thought they would be filming in July 2010 and planned a New Zealand tour of his play, *Waiting for Godot*, so that as soon as it wrapped, he would be ready to start, but filming was delayed.

Back in May 2008, both Peter Jackson and Guillermo del Toro were asked in a live webchat how they envisaged Gandalf's role in *The Hobbit* movies. The web host commented: 'He seems to go off on his own and disappear in several sections of the book. Do you want to stay faithful to that, or give him a more active role?' Del Toro replied: 'I believe that Gandalf is meant to be used in that way – coming and going, in and out of the narrative. If anything, this creates the perfect setting for those "gaps" to be bridged by the second film.'

Jackson added: 'Those gaps are great! There's a lot of stuff going on, which is distracting him. I'm just pleased to be getting Gandalf the Grey back for two more movies. Ian and I loved him best – we were a little sad when Gandy the White took over.'

DID YOU KNOW?

Ian McKellen was given permission by Guillermo del Toro to read the script for the first movie and then the second movie in 2010. The other actors had to wait a long time before they received just a handful of pages but del Toro knew that he could trust him to keep what he had read a secret.

Del Toro later told McKellen why he was stepping down as director: he was concerned about scheduling and he needed to do other projects as well. Sir Ian revealed all in his blog.

After it was announced that filming would start in February 2011, with Peter Jackson as director, Sir Ian started to question whether he should after all play Gandalf. He explained what happened in a blog post, writing: 'I kept wondering, was Gandalf what I most wanted to do, more than a new play, for instance or indeed a new part? Sequels aren't necessarily as rewarding to act in as their originals.

'Could I let Gandalf go? Would anyone else care if I did? Elsewhere, does anyone care that Michael Gambon was not the first to play Dumbledore?

'The deciding negotiation was not about money but about dates. Gandalf is needed on set over the next 18 months, but with sizeable breaks when I can work on other projects. My worry that I could not easily escape from Middle-earth was lifted.'

Thankfully, Sir Ian decided to continue playing Gandalf, even when the start date was pushed back another month to 28 March 2011. Everyone had been ready to begin, but Peter Jackson needed to have an urgent stomach operation because he had a perforated ulcer. His insurance company were demanding that he took five weeks off to recover and so he had no choice. He couldn't even attend a press conference, leaving a representative to read out the following statement to journalists: 'I'd love to be with you all this morning, but I'm currently under a medical form of house arrest, to prevent me from overdoing it until fully recovered from my recent operation. I'll be jumping back into it very soon and to be honest, the guys that you'll be talking to this morning make me laugh so hard, right now I'd be in danger of popping a few stitches.'

Once the director was back, Sir Ian started filming his scenes with Martin Freeman and the dwarf actors at Bilbo's home. During shooting, Jackson admitted to *Entertainment Weekly*: 'He's in fantastic form. In a way, his role in *The Hobbit* has more technical difficulties than *The Lord of the Rings* did, because he has scenes with 14 smaller characters – obviously the dwarves and the Hobbit are shorter. I remember saying to him, "Look, this isn't

Waiting For Godot or *King Lear*. This is *The Hobbit* – this is the real thing." '

Glóin

- Name: Glóin
- Alias: None
- Race: Dwarf of the House of Durin
- Played by: Peter Hambleton
- Character description: Glóin is a dwarf with a white hood. He is the brother of Oin and they are distant cousins of Thorin. Both are talented fire starters. Glóin is married and has a son called Gimli (who appears in the *Lord of the Rings* movies).

The actor chosen to play Glóin was Peter Hambleton. Peter is a Kiwi actor and learnt his craft at New Zealand Drama School. He is also a talented theatre director, and throughout his career, he has worked in radio, stage, television and movies. Altogether, he has appeared in over 70 professional theatre productions in New Zealand and is a Circa Theatre Council Member. He is married, with a son called Joseph and a daughter called Sophie, who has followed in his footsteps and is now an actress.

In a press conference, he talked about how the dwarves had bonded in rehearsals, even before filming began: 'It's a great bunch of guys – we feel like a bunch of mates already. We're all strong personalities, but we're all equal and we get on well together.'

In one of the production blogs Peter joked: 'I think when people see the beards, beards are gonna come back in big time!'

On Day 18 of *The Hobbit* shoot, Peter was filming some scenes in Bilbo's home with the other dwarves when the actor John Rhys-Davies dropped by. John played Gimli in *The Lord of the Rings* movies, so it was especially nice for Peter to meet him because Gimli is Glóin's son.

DID YOU KNOW?

Playing a dwarf in *The Lord of the Rings* was a terrible ordeal for John because he was extremely allergic to the prosthetics used on his face, which resulted in his skin peeling off and painful blisters.

Gollum

- Name: Gollum
- Alias: My Precious
- Race: Hobbit of (or related to) the Stoor branch
- Played by: Andy Serkis
- Character description: Gollum is a slimy creature, small in stature. He has a thin face and large, pale eyes.

DID YOU KNOW?

In the first edition of *The Hobbit*, Tolkien had Gollum planning to give Bilbo his ring as a prize for winning the riddles, before realising that it was missing. He then showed Bilbo the exit. Tolkien decided to change it for the second edition, which was published in 1951 so that it would fit with *The Lord of the Rings* plot.

The actor chosen to play Gollum in *The Hobbit* (and *The Lord of the Rings*) movies was Andy Serkis. He is a British actor, having been born in Ruislip Manor, London. Andy's father was from the Republic of Armenia and worked as a medical doctor in Iraq while his son was growing up. Until he was ten, Andy spent a lot of time going back and forth from London to Baghdad.

As a youngster, Andy didn't want to become an actor; he wanted to be an artist and thought he would be involved in set design or something artistic behind the scenes. He learnt all about set building and design at Lancaster University, where he studied Visual Arts. While there, he was asked whether he would appear in a play his fellow students were putting on, to which he agreed, not knowing it would change his life. As soon as he was on stage in Barrie Keefe's play *Gotcha*, he realised that he wanted to be an actor, not a set designer.

He explained to Orange: 'Painting was my thing, so I wanted to be a painter or a graphic designer. And I went to Lancaster University to do that, and also because it was near the Lake District and climbing was a big hobby of mine as well. But I didn't realise that you had to do another subject in your first year and I didn't know what I was going to do. But there was a really good theatre studies department, so I thought it was arts related and decided to get involved with that. I started designing some posters for them, and sets and things like that but then I started acting in productions until I played this one role which was huge epiphany moment in my life, where it was "This is what I've got to do." '

After finishing university, Andy decided to stay in Lancaster and started acting in productions at the Duke's Playhouse. He wanted to learn on the job rather than by spending more years studying at university or acting college. During an interview with WhatsOnStage.com in 2001, he was asked what his first big break was. He replied: '*Privates on Parade*, directed by Jonathan Petherbridge at the Duke's Playhouse in Lancaster. I joined the local rep at the Duke's Playhouse and did about 14 productions over a year and a half – that's where I got my equity card and learnt my craft as an actor.'

He went on to work with touring theatre companies, the Royal Exchange Theatre in Manchester and London's Royal Court Theatre. In 1987, he broke into television and made his movie debut in the 1994 film *Royal Deceit*, starring Christian Bale and Kate Beckinsale. Five years later, he would get his biggest break, playing Gollum in the first *The Lord of the Rings* movie. He very nearly missed out, though, as he explained to the Sabotage Times: 'When the role was first offered to me, I wasn't that interested in it. At that time I was simply asked whether I'd like to provide the voice of a character for a film that was going to be shot in New Zealand and that didn't have a lot of appeal. But then it emerged that the film in question was *The Lord of the Rings*, that the director was Peter Jackson and that the part was Gollum. When all of that had been established, I was much more curious, but I still wasn't that interested in simply sitting in a booth and providing the vocals. So then I started talking to Peter and his wife and collaborator, Fran Walsh, and we reached a point where we agreed that it would be more interesting if I interpreted the part on set. I'm so glad we did that because I think that Gollum wouldn't work so well without that direct interaction with Elijah Wood and Sean Astin.'

Andy spent two years wearing a skin-tight CGI (computer generated imagery) suit with markers so that cameras could pick up each move he made for the three *The Lord of the Rings* movies; he had to do the same for *The Hobbit* films. During a *Lord of the Rings* interview, CBBC viewer Sylvie asked him: 'How long compared to a normal scene does it take to make a scene as Gollum, for you as an actor?'

Andy replied: 'That's a good question because we shoot everything as you would in normal film and then it goes through a whole lot of processes. I have to re-shoot everything again in a motion capture studio and then I have to work with the animators and then re-voice everything. So all in all, the process can take, with the animating process as well, some scenes have taken two and a half years to make.'

> **DID YOU KNOW?**
>
> To create Gollum's voice, Andy copied the sound his cats made when coughing up fur balls. He explained in an interview for CBBC: 'I was looking at my cat and I saw that when they got fur balls in the back of their throats, their whole bodies convulsed and then they made this kind of coughing sound and that seemed to be right for the way that Gollum says – when he actually says Gollum, Gollum, it absolutely fitted it perfectly.'

In the gap between *The Lord of the Rings* movies and *The Hobbit*, Andy played more CGI-driven characters, as well as traditional characters. He played Kong in the 2005 blockbuster *King Kong*, magazine boss Richard Kneeland in *13 Going on 30*, Alley in *The Prestige* and was the voice of Spike in *Flushed Away*. In his spare time, he likes to paint and enjoys climbing mountains.

For *The Hobbit* movies Andy was the second unit director and he enjoyed being in Martin Freeman's first-ever scene as Bilbo. He believed it was good to start with the chamber piece but felt like he was doing an impersonation for the first few days.

FILM FACT:

Andy Serkis was the first actor in the make-up chair on the first day of *The Hobbit* filming.

Once Andy had shot his scenes in the chamber, he was done as an actor because Gollum has only a small part in *The Hobbit* and so he was able to spend the rest of the time directing. He told the *Hollywood Reporter*: 'I think I understand Peter's sensibility and we have a common history of understanding Middle-earth. A lot of the crew from *The Lord of the Rings* was returning to work on *The Hobbit*. There is really a sense of Peter wanting people around him who totally understand the material and the work ethic.'

In another interview, this time with IGN, Andy discussed how he became second unit director. He said: 'Peter asked me to get involved, and he's known that I've wanted to direct for many years because we've obviously spent a lot of time with each other over the last decade, so I was thrilled to be asked and he just said, "I want you to take it and run and be bold and make great decisions, and you know 2nd unit director on a project of that scale is vast, it's huge 'cos it encompasses drama as well as battle sequences and vistas, and it's really varied." '

When filming *The Hobbit*, Andy was away from his wife, Lorraine Ashbourne, and his three children, Ruby, Sonny and Louis (they had to remain in England because of school). He explained to Orange Film at the time: 'They're coming out for the summer holidays and Christmas holidays and Easter holidays, but they're starting secondary school now and sadly that is the major downer of the whole thing – being away for long periods of time. But we have Skype, so I've had some interesting Skype moments where I'm cooking dinner in the evening and they're all having breakfast and I can hear them all screaming. I just imagine myself being at home. But I have to be there virtually – a virtual dad [laughs].'

Andy has set up his own studio in London called The

Imaginarium with producer Jonathan Cavendish. They specialise in performance capture. Asked by James Peaty from Den of Geek how it was coming along in August 2011, he revealed: 'We're fully invested now and, at the moment, we're putting together the technology and the crew, and we should be up and running early next year. Part of our remit is that we're a producing studio so we've got two films, a TV series idea and a live theatre show that we're developing. But then there's also the academy side and the R&D element, where we're trying to both further the technology, as well as teach the necessary techniques to young acting students.'

Great Goblin

- Name: Great Goblin
- Alias: None
- Race: Orc (Goblin)
- Played by: CGI character – computer generated imagery (played by Barry Humphries)
- Character description: The Great Goblin is a large goblin with a large head. He is an important ruler.

The actor chosen to voice the Great Goblin was Barry Humphries. He was born in Kew, Melbourne, Australia. Barry is multi-talented: as well as being an actor, he is a comedian, scriptwriter, artist, film producer and author. He is best known for his alter ego, Dame Edna Everage.

Director Peter Jackson announced Barry's casting on his Facebook page. He wrote: 'I'm also highly excited that Barry Humphries will be portraying the Goblin King, in much the way Andy Serkis created Gollum. Barry is perhaps best known for his business and social connections as the long-time manager of Dame Edna Everage. He has also been an ardent supporter of the rather misunderstood and unfairly maligned Australian politician, Sir Les Patterson. However, in his spare time, Barry is also a fine actor, and we're looking forward to seeing him invest the Goblin King with the delicate sensitivity and emotional depth this character deserves.'

While being interviewed by the New Zealand Prime Minister John Key, Jackson was asked if the goblins are well behaved. He replied: 'They're kind of well behaved. I mean, sort of have to give them air – we got compressed air hoses and we stick this air down their suits every now and again to give them a breath of fresh air and then keep them going. But yeah, they're small and mischievous and rather evil.'

He also talked about what shooting was like, saying: 'The good thing about making a movie is that you don't ever have two days that are the same – for instance, yesterday we spent all day in the middle of a storm. We had thunder, lightning, rain – we had dwarves walking up a rocky path on the side of a cliff, so we spent all day with dwarves being drenched in water, which was kind of fun. They didn't enjoy it that much – and today we show up and we've got flame, fire and goblins – so every single day is different, so you can't relax. You sort of come to work each day and you're right in the thick of problems and difficulties and everything else, which is well, it certainly makes it interesting.'

Horses

When the dwarves, Bilbo and Gandalf go on their quest they all ride ponies apart from Gandalf, who rides a white horse. The dwarves in the book are very small but for the full-sized actors riding ponies would be a problem as they would look ridiculous and the ponies would struggle to carry them. To solve this, director Peter Jackson had the actors ride horses, disguised to look like ponies (they each had shaggy jackets and from a distance, this made them look like ponies).

The scene where Bilbo rejoins the group on the outskirts of The Shire was filmed at Ohakune Beech

Paddock, a wooded area. For this, the actors had all spent many months practising horse riding and so were pretty experienced horse riders, but with 15 horses being ridden at once there were plenty of opportunities for things to go wrong. The horses all had to feel completely comfortable so their trainers made sure they got to sniff the boom mics and other equipment before filming started. One shot Peter wanted to get was of Bilbo being picked up by Fili and Kili and put on a horse. This was tricky because the actors playing Fili and Kili would be on horseback themselves at the time.

Stunt coordinator Glenn Boswell figured out what needed to be done, so the crew and cast members moved to a flatter piece of land away from all the trees so it would be simpler. They put a box on the ground at the point where Dean O'Gorman (Fili) and Aidan Turner (Kili) would pick Martin Freeman up, so he had something he could push up on. This would make it a whole lot easier for them and would also look good on camera. They just had to lift him up for the shot because the stunt Bilbo could be used later when it came to putting him on the actual horse. If they had tried it with Martin, he might have injured himself because it's quite tricky.

As well as horses, there were other animals in the cast. Steve Old was the Lead Animal Wrangler on set and he was in charge of looking after all the animals and checking that they were OK as they moved from location to location. Steve works for FarOut Events Limited and was horse coordinator for *The Lord of the Rings* movies.

He told the backstage camera that he had 'Michael Jackson the walking chicken on a lead, 49 sheep, 50 chickens, nine goats, five cows, four pheasants, two ducks all going out on location. For the market scenes in Hobbiton there was a enormous pig waddling about.'

Itaril

Some Tolkien fans were left feeling slightly miffed when they read the casting call information for an actress to play Itaril:

ITARIL – female, a woodland Elf, this character is one of the Silvan Elves. The Silvan Elves are seen as more earthy and practical. Shorter than other elves, she is still quick and lithe and physically adept, being able to fight with both sword and bow. Showing promise as a fighter at a young age, ITARIL was chosen to train to become part of the Woodland

King's Guard. This is the only life she has ever expected to live, until she meets and secretly falls in love with a young ELF LORD. This role will require a wig and contact lenses to be worn. Some prosthetic make-up may also be required. LEAD. AGE: 17–27.

They didn't like the fact that director Peter Jackson was trying to bring in more female characters. Fan Brian Murphy summed it up in a comment that he left on theblogthattimeforgot. He said: 'I really wish Jackson/Walsh/Boyens would quit pandering. Yes, *The Hobbit* was entirely men. So what? It's a great book that requires no modification.'

Other fans vowed to wait and see. Guilemaster on the website Middle-Earth Center, commented: 'I'll give Peter Jackson the benefit of the doubt. I've come to trust him as a director; I know he will do it better than everyone else. It should also be noted that the two movies aren't simply based on *The Hobbit* book alone. They will also contain events that occur between *The Lord of the Rings* and *The Hobbit*.'

Irish actress Saoirse Ronan won the part but later had to drop out because of other filming commitments. Previously she had played the lead role of Susie in Jackson's 2009 movie, *The Lovely Bones*. In an interview with the *Belfast Telegraph*, she said: 'It's probably not going to work out with *The Hobbit*, unfortunately because I would have been working for about a year on it and there were other projects that I was very interested in, but Pete and Fran have been very good about it and very understanding. I'll have to just go back down to New Zealand for a holiday and hang out with the hobbits.'

There was no further news about the part and fans felt that maybe Jackson had decided not to include Itaril after all.

My precious. Andy Serkis
reprises his role as
Gollum for *The Hobbit*.
©*Getty Images*

Above: Legendary director Peter Jackson: the man behind *The Lord of the Rings* and *The Hobbit* movies.   *©Getty Images*

Below: Middle Earth: *The Hobbit*'s film set in Matamata, Waikato, New Zealand.   *©Rex Features*

Above and Below: An aerial view of the film set: Hobbiton.   ©*Rex Features*

Flying the flag for Britain.

Above left: British actor Martin Freeman takes on the role of Bilbo
Baggins, the films' protagonist.   ©*Getty Images*

Above right: Irish-born actor Aidan Turner plays Kili, one of the thirteen
dwarves. Among the other dwarf actors he is affectionately known as the
'sexy dwarf'.   ©*Getty Images*

Below left: Fellow Irish actor James Nesbitt plays Bofur the dwarf. Apart
from Billy Connolly, James is arguably the funniest member of the cast.
©*Getty Images*

Below right: The voice of Smaug the dragon: Benedict Cumberbatch.
©*Getty Images*

Above left: Stephen Fry plays the Master of Lake-town. Fry is said to have thoroughly enjoyed playing a character that is 'an unappetising piece of work'.   *©Getty Images*

Above right: English actor Ian McKellan reprised his role as Gandalf . His scenes are apparently more technically challenging because he has to be filmed with fourteen smaller characters.   *©Getty Images*

Below left: Scottish actor and comedian Billy Connolly plays Dain Ironfoot.
                                                                         ©Getty Images

Below right: Fellow Scottish actor Ken Stott (Balin the dwarf).
                                                                         ©Getty Images

Above left: Bret Mckenzie plays the elf Lindir. McKenzie played elf Figwit, an extra, in the first *Lord of the Rings* film, and gained such a large online following that he was invited back. *©Getty Images*

Above right: Australian comedian Barry Humphries voices the Great Goblin. *©Getty Images*

Below left: American actor Lee Pace plays the Elvenking Thranduil. *©Getty Images*

Below right: Luke Evans was cast to play Bard, an archer of Lake-town who kills Smaug. *©Getty Images*

Although they don't feature in JRR Tolkien's book *The Hobbit*, Peter Jackson made the decision to include new characters and reintroduce existing characters from *The Lord of the Rings*.

Above left: Orlando Bloom. Peter Jackson considered his portrayal of Legolas to be 'iconic' and was keen for him to return.   *©Getty Images*

Above right: Elijah Wood (Frodo Baggins).   *©Getty Images*

Below left: Evangeline Lilly was chosen to play the new character Tauriel, the head of the Elven guard in Mirkwood.   *©Getty Images*

Below right: Cate Blanchett (Galadriel, elf Lady of Lórien) appeared in *The Lord of the Rings*.   *©Getty Images*

Above: Some of the key actors at a *Hobbit* press conference.   ©Getty Image

Below: Being briefed.   ©Getty Image

J

Jabez Olssen

Jabez Olssen was the editor for *The Hobbit* movies. Previously, he had edited *The Lord of the Rings: The Two Towers* with Mike Horton. Jabez is from Dunedin, New Zealand and was also the editor for Peter Jackson's movie, *The Lovely Bones*, the TV series *Cleopatra 2525* and the shorts, *Crossing the Line* and *Fog*.

In 2003 he won the Best Editing Award at the Online Film Critics Society Awards and the Best Editing Award at the Las Vegas Film Critics Society Awards. Both of these awards were shared with his fellow *Two Towers* editor Mike Horton. He was also nominated for a

BAFTA but sadly lost out to Daniel Rezende, who edited *City of God*.

Jabez trained at South Seas Film School, graduating in 1998. He began his professional career at the prestigious production company Silverscreen and learnt how to use the latest editing equipment. Following this, he worked on the TV show *Jack of all Trades*, adding 60 visual effects to each episode, and edited TV adverts. His big break came when he was recommended by someone for a job on *The Lord of the Rings*. Peter Jackson needed an avid editor with sfx (special effects) post-production skills, and when interviewed, Jabez proved to be the right person for the job. For him, it was a dream come true.

Mike Horton was editing *The Lord of the Rings: The Two Towers* with Peter Jackson when Jabez began work as an assistant. He was so keen and skilled that he impressed everyone and Mike decided to let him share the editing role – quite remarkable really because he didn't have to do this. Once the work ended, Jabez found himself working on more movie projects for Jackson and become editor of *The Lovely Bones* and *The Hobbit* movies.

During a webchat, Peter Jackson was asked by fans if there would be extended editions of *The Hobbit* movies and he replied: 'The truth (and this is the truth) is that you don't plan for extended editions up front. An extended edition is the result of leftover scenes that have been deleted out of theatrical cut. In an ideal world the script is written lean and tight and therefore there are no scenes left on the cutting-room floor and therefore no extended edition. However, when writing three epic *The Lord of the Rings* films there was no way we could keep the writing process as lean, so the extended edition was a result of seeing our thought process during the writing and shooting play itself out onscreen with scenes we no longer needed when we finally cut the films together. Whether there will be an extended edition of *The Hobbit* will depend entirely on the final theatrical cut and what we have left over.'

Even though Jackson didn't confirm this, fans predicted there would be extended editions of both movies released on DVD and Blu-ray.

Kili

- Name: Kili
- Alias: None
- Race: Dwarf of the House of Durin
- Played by: Aidan Turner
- Character description: Kili is a young dwarf with a yellow beard, silver belt and blue hood. He plays the fiddle. When Bilbo first meets him, he is carrying a spade and a bag of tools. He is the brother of Fili and they are the nephews of Thorin.

> ### DID YOU KNOW?
>
> Tolkien devised Kili's name from the old Scandinavian poem, *Völuspá*. The poem was written by the poet Edda and is about the creation and destruction of the world.

The actor chosen to play Kili was Aidan Turner. Aidan is an Irish actor, who was born in Clondalkin and grew up in Tallaght, Ireland. Internationally, he is best known for playing vampire John Mitchell in the BBC3 series *Being Human* and Bedoli in the TV series *The Tudors*. In Ireland he is best known for playing Ruairí McGowanre in the medical drama *The Clinic*.

Aidan has acted in movies before but on a much smaller scale. He played John Schofield in the TV movie *Hattie* (2011) and Theodoro in the 2007 short film *Matterhorn*.

> ### DID YOU KNOW?
>
> Aidan really wanted to go skiing while living in New Zealand but he didn't think that he'd be allowed to do so in case he injured himself.

The other dwarf actors liked trying to wind Aidan up. James Nesbitt (who plays Bofur) joked: 'Aidan Turner, he's the sexy dwarf. I don't even think he's got a beard, actually. Mainly because he's not old enough to grow one.'

Legolas

- Name: Legolas
- Alias: Legolas Greenleaf
- Race: Sindarin Elf (although presents himself as a Silvan Elf)
- Played by: Orlando Bloom
- Description: Legolas is tall and fair with bright eyes. He dresses in green and brown and is a skilled archer.

The actor chosen to play Legolas in *The Hobbit* and *The Lord of the Rings* movies was Orlando Bloom. At first, fans were disappointed to hear that Legolas would be featuring in *The Hobbit* movies because he doesn't appear in the book, but Peter Jackson reassured them that it would be done in a fitting way. The director wrote on his Facebook page: 'Ten years ago, Orlando Bloom created an iconic character with his portrayal of Legolas.

'I'm excited to announce today that we'll be revisiting Middle-earth with him once more. I'm thrilled to be working with Orlando again. Funny thing is, I look older – and he doesn't! I guess that's why he makes such a wonderful elf.'

Orlando is a British actor from Canterbury, Kent. When he was four, the man he believed to be his dad, Harry Bloom, died of a stroke. Orlando and his sister Samantha were raised by their mother Sonia and a family friend called Colin Stone. When he was thirteen, Orlando was told that Colin was in fact his biological dad.

At school Orlando loved being in plays and after watching the movie *The Hustler* one Christmas, he decided he wanted to be like Paul Newman – he wanted to be an actor. He joined a community theatre group and took part in poetry and Bible reciting competitions with his sister, which they often won.

DID YOU KNOW?

Orlando Bloom's first job was at a pigeon shooting range as a clay trapper.

When he turned sixteen, Orlando moved to London and enrolled in the National Youth Theatre. He was so talented that he got a scholarship for the British American Drama Academy. Following this, he started out with bit parts in the TV shows *Midsomer Murders*, *Casualty* and *Smack the Pony*. His first movie role was in the 1997 movie *Wilde*, starring Stephen Fry, Jude Law and Michael Sheen.

Orlando was always keen to learn as much as he could in order to become a better actor and he enrolled in the Guildhall School of Music & Drama. In 1998, while studying, he had a terrible accident and fell from a rooftop terrace, breaking his back. Quite remarkably, he made a full recovery and was soon back on stage with his fellow students. The next year, Peter Jackson saw him perform and afterwards asked him to audition for *The Lord of the Rings*. His audition was successful and the part of Legolas was his. On graduating, he then moved to New Zealand with the rest of the cast to start filming.

FILM FACT

Orlando has a tattoo on his right wrist, which is the word 'nine' written in Tengwar (Elvish) script. This symbolises the fact that Legolas was one of nine members of The Fellowship of the Ring.

Orlando Bloom wasn't the only cast member to get a

tattoo symbolising the nine members of The Fellowship
of the Ring. All of the other members got the same tattoo,
apart from John Rhys-Davies (Gimli). John's stunt double
got the tattoo instead! They chatted to the *LOTR* fan club
magazine about who did the tattoos.

Dominic Monaghan (Meriadoc) confessed: 'It was a
guy called Roger at Roger's Tattoo Parlour in Wellington.
He didn't open on Sunday, but we only had a day off on
a Sunday. After we all came together and committed to
this idea, I think Viggo rang him. He told him, "We know
you don't open on a Sunday, we'll make it worth your
while." We all turned up there, I think at 11:00, and it was
a real party atmosphere. We were all taking photos and
writing in diaries. It was one of my favourite days in New
Zealand, I think. I'll show you [mine] because these guys
have theirs on their foot. [Lifts shirt up to show his
shoulder blade.]'

Billy Boyd (Pippin) added: 'Of course, we got the
tattoos about a week before we finished [shooting],
and I wasn't really thinking ahead, so we still had a week
to [spend with] these prosthetic feet! And I had the
tattoo and so did Sean. They had to glue [the feet] on –
quite painful.'

Sir Ian McKellen was surprised that he had one done
because he never thought he would have a tattoo. During
an interview with chat show host Michael Parkinson, he

confessed that they visited a tattoo parlour and revealed that his tattoo is on his shoulder.

When Orlando arrived to film *The Hobbit* he recognised lots of the crew as many of them had previously worked on *The Lord of the Rings* movies. He was surprised how easy it was to get back into character, revealing to Collider.com in October 2011: 'It's crazy, the wig fits. It still fits. It's the same wig, and it still fits. And the costume, it fits. The same costume fits. I'm not actually wearing – well, I'm not gonna talk about it, I can't tell you anything else.'

Lindir

- Name: Lindir
- Alias: None
- Race: Rivendell Elf
- Played by: Bret McKenzie
- Character description: Lindir is a Rivendell Elf who doesn't actually appear in *The Hobbit* book but is in chapter one, entitled 'Many Meetings', in the book *The Fellowship of the Ring*.

The actor chosen to play Lindir was Bret McKenzie. Bret is an actor from Wellington, New Zealand. In the first and third of *The Lord of the Rings* movies he played Figwit, an elf. He had no lines in the first movie as he was just an extra but he gained thousands of fans online and was given a line for the third movie. Peter McKenzie, his dad, played Elendil in the prologue. To find out more about Figwit, go to www.figwitlives.net. On the website is the explanation of how Figwit got his name: 'When Frodo says "I will take it!" we are so impressed we start to think "Frodo is great!" But before we finish, the camera pans and we see Figwit, smouldering enigmatically in the background. All other thoughts are whisked away by that elf – who is THAT?! He's gorgeous!'

Once Bret was cast, Ian McKellen wrote in his blog: 'Another slim-line elf returning from *LOTR* is a local: New Zealand's actor/comedian/singer Bret McKenzie. Last time, he was an extra at Rivendell, the elven Last Homely House in the East. Under a tree at the Council of Elrond, he silently witnessed the forming of the Fellowship. Wordless maybe but not unnoticed by fans of the beautiful, who gave him the acronym F.I.G.W.I.T. ('Frodo Is Great! Who Is That?') I confess Gandalf didn't take much notice, distracted by the main action that involved all the main characters.'

As well as acting, Bret is also a keen musician and was an original member of the band, The Black Seeds. He released a solo album in 2009 called *Prototype*. Together with his friend Jemaine Clement, they are the Grammy

Award-winning comedy duo, The Flight of the Conchords and have a worldwide cult following. Bret won an Oscar for a song he wrote for *The Muppets* (2011), while Jemaine has been nominated for an Emmy in the past.

DID YOU KNOW?

Bret and Jemaine have starred in an episode of *The Simpsons*. If you want to check them out, you need to watch the season premiere of the 22nd season (series) titled 'Elementary School Musical'.

Lobelia Sackville-Baggins

- Name: Lobelia Sackville-Baggins
- Alias: Old Hagling
- Race: Hobbit
- Played by: Unknown, not listed as a movie character
- Character description: Lobelia Sackville-Baggins is Bilbo's cousin and he thinks that she probably stole his spoons while he was away on his quest. She carries an umbrella.

Locations

One of the reasons people loved *The Lord of the Rings*

movies was because of the great New Zealand landscapes and locations used, and for *The Hobbit* movies, director Peter Jackson and his team wanted to make sure that the landscapes and locations were just as good, if not better. Jared Connon was hired as supervising location manager and worked with a large team to scout the best locations, get permission to shoot there, make the changes needed, watch over everything and, once filming finished, sort out what needed to be done next. He had started his career as a location assistant in the 1990s on the TV series *High Tide* and the movies *Heaven* and *The Chosen*. His first job as a location manager had been on the first *The Lord of the Rings* film and he has worked with Peter Jackson many times since, on the other *The Lord of the Rings* movies, *The Lovely Bones* and *King Kong*.

Jared needed to know what sort of locations were required for *The Hobbit* and then once he found somewhere he thought was perfect, he had to figure out if it was accessible enough. With hundreds of crewmembers due to descend on the different locations, he had to decide if the roads were suitable and if there was room enough for all the tents and Portaloos.

On the 5th production video, he admitted: 'The main reason for going on location on the project is to capture the scenic beauty of New Zealand. Peter has often said one of the things that won the fans over so much in *The*

Lord of the Rings series was the unbelievable vistas and scenics because they were so magnificent.'

He continued: 'You have to take everything with you. The daunting aspect of it is it's all got to get onto trucks, it's all got to be on wheels. It's all got to be ready to roll. One of our biggest challenges on the production is actually shooting all of the locations in one hit for both main unit and second unit.'

Peter Jackson also commented: 'We've been travelling pretty much the length and breadth of New Zealand, shooting locations for *The Hobbit*. It's been great to get outside; it's been great to get that texture of Middle-earth into the movie after many, many weeks of shooting in the studio. We've established our characters, we've established our story and it was finally time to get on the road and establish the landscapes of Middle-earth.'

DID YOU KNOW?

The team had shot in a studio for 110 days before they went out on location!

When the crews had to move, this involved a lot of organisation. Peter's crew was 500-strong, while Andy's crew was 200-strong. The person in charge of making it happen as smoothly as possible was unit production manager, Brigitte Yorke. She had her work cut out, though, as there were roughly 140 trucks and other vehicles involved each time. Production supervisor Stephie Weststrate was also in charge of organising everybody.

Jared was actually hired while Guillermo del Toro was the director but many of the locations he chose were still used once Peter Jackson became director. He has a great understanding of Middle-earth and in the beginning of the process he would pore over the script and make a list of the different types of locations needed. At first he did this with Guillermo and then with Peter; they would tell him what they were planning to shoot on location and what would take place in the studio. Members of the location team would then travel in helicopters around the whole of New Zealand, taking photographs of potential places and then everyone would meet up, have a look at the photos and decide which ones looked most promising. Even if Jared was confident that a location was just right, he still had to have the director and various bosses come along and see for themselves before arranging contracts with landowners. Every location had to be just what Peter was looking for.

Some fans make the mistake that things are filmed in chronological order but this is not the case. Directors will shoot scenes in any order at all and when it comes to location shooting, they will film as many different ones in the same location as possible because it saves time and money. When filming in Hobbiton, they filmed the day Bilbo goes on the quest one day and the very next day, they filmed him coming back!

The locations block of filming lasted approximately seven and a half weeks and the first location was Matamata.

DID YOU KNOW?

When they visited the town of Te Kuiti there were not enough hotels in the small town to accommodate all the cast and crew so the towns-people gave up their own homes so the cast and crew had somewhere to sleep.

Peter and Andy spent a lot of time apart, shooting in different locations. During one of the production videos, Andy and his team revealed all. Andy admitted: 'I've spent quite a lot of the last few weeks in a chopper because a lot of our stuff was aerial coverage. We'd take off and choose our line, and choose the way we were going to shoot it and how we were going to reveal the landscapes.'

Liz Tan, the second unit first assistant director, added: 'The bonuses of being on second unit is we do a lot of locations that are too tricky or time consuming for the main unit to go to, so a lot of our locations are helicopter-only access. We've got very good at loading in and out of choppers.'

The two units only met up halfway through the location shoot, which, coincidently, was the halfway point for the whole shoot of the two movies: Day 127, 10 November 2011. To celebrate, Peter gave all the crewmembers a commemorative hoodie. He had done the same thing at the halfway point when shooting *The Lord of the Rings* movies. Back then the halfway point had been Day 133, 23 May 2000. In the production video, Peter joked that it's taken them longer to shoot the two movies because they are all 10 years older (the announcement that there were going to be three movies, rather than the two planned, was made in July 2012).

Andy wanted to keep Peter informed on what unit 2 had done each day so he made a little edit and then sent it to the director. Because of the remoteness of some of the locations, satellites had to be set up to provide the much-needed Internet.

Lord of the Eagles
- Name: Lord of the Eagles
- Alias: Mighty Eagle, the Great Eagles, King of All Birds
- Race: Eagles of the Northern Mountains
- Played by: Unknown

- Character description: The Great Eagles are the greatest of birds. They are honest and noble, with great hunting skills. In the past, Gandalf had saved the Lord of the Eagles from an arrow injury so the Lord of the Eagles helps him, Bilbo and the dwarves to escape the wolves and goblins.

The Lord of the Rings

The Lord of the Rings movies were released in 2001, 2002 and 2003. They were based on the J.R.R. Tolkien books, first published in 1954–55. When interviewed by GreenCine back in December 2002, Peter Jackson said: 'There are certainly themes Tolkien felt were important. We made a promise to ourselves at the beginning of the process that we weren't going to put any of our own politics, our own messages or our own themes into these movies. What we were trying to do was to analyse what was important to Tolkien and to try to honour that. In a way, we were trying to make these films for him, not for ourselves.'

The first movie was called *The Lord of the Rings: The Fellowship of the Ring*, the second was *The Lord of the Rings: The Two Towers* and the third was *The Return of the King*. All three films were directed by Peter Jackson and distributed by New Line Cinema. Like *The Hobbit*, they were filmed in New Zealand. The first movie made $871 million worldwide, the second made $926 million and the third took over $1 billion, making *The Lord of the Rings* the seventh highest-grossing movie series ever.

Here is the Top 10:
- *Harry Potter*
- *James Bond*
- *Star Wars*
- *Pirates of the Caribbean*
- *Marvel Cinematic Universe*
- *Shrek*
- *The Lord of the Rings*
- *Transformers*
- *Batman*
- *The Twilight Saga*

Each of the movies in the trilogy was nominated for numerous Oscars, with *The Lord of the Rings: The Return of the King* picking up the most. It received 11 out of the 11 awards for which it was nominated. *The Lord of the Rings: The Fellowship of the Ring* picked up four out of a possible 13, while *The Lord of the Rings: The Two Towers* achieved two out of a possible six.

Peter Jackson first read *The Lord of the Rings* books when he was a teenager after seeing the 1978 animated movie. He had 12 hours to kill on a train as he travelled to Auckland from Wellington, so had plenty of time to read it all. As he glanced out the window he couldn't help but think that the New Zealand landscapes looked very similar to Middle-earth.

Originally, he planned for there to be two movies instead of three and spent 14 months writing the first scripts with his partner Fran Walsh, Philippa Boyens and Stephen Sinclair (Stephen later withdraw because of other commitments). After Miramax came to the conclusion that the budget wouldn't stretch to two movies, it was suggested that revisions should be made so that it was just one film. Peter hated this idea and went to meet with other studios. During a meeting with New Line Cinema, co-founder Bob Shaye asked why they were making two movies instead of three as Tolkien's original story had been published in three volumes. They were willing to make the movies, so long as there were three!

Sadly Peter's mother, Joan, died just three days before *The Lord of the Rings: The Fellowship of the Ring* came out.

DID YOU KNOW?

For *The Lord of the Rings* movies Weta Workshop had to make 500 bows and 10,000 arrows! There were also 48,000 individual pieces of armour to be crafted.

> ### FILM FACT
> Nineteen thousand different costumes were used in the three movies!

> ### FILM FACT
> For *The Lord of the Rings* movies, 1,800 pairs of hobbit feet had been made and because of the long time from the final movie to *The Hobbit* shooting, the art department had to start from scratch.

When Peter Jackson is filming a movie he is so busy that he hardly gets any sleep at all. He usually manages about four hours a night as he has so much to do every day.

Some of the special effects in *The Lord of the Rings* movies had never been seen before. In total, there were 2,730 special effects over the three movies, which required the skills of hundreds of visual effects artists.

Peter Jackson used different editors for each movie. For *The Lord of the Rings: The Fellowship of the Ring*, he hired John Gilbert; Mike Horton and Jabez Olssen edited *The Lord of the Rings: The Two Towers* and Jamie Selkirk and Annie Collins worked on *The Return of the King*. A decade later he hired Jabez Olssen to be the editor of *The Hobbit* movies.

At the start of the second movie the studio wanted the director to include a flashback of what had happened in

SARAH OLIVER

the first movie in case any of the audience hadn't already seen it. He hated that idea and told IGN movies: 'It was just a logical decision, really. I kind of figured that, you know: how many people are going to see *The Two Towers* who haven't seen *The Fellowship of the Ring*? Obviously there will be some, because there's always going to be some people that sort of show up and wonder why they're confused [he laughs]. I just figured there's no reason for that because *The Fellowship of the Ring* is out on DVD now. And you know, you don't have to go buy one, you've probably got a friend who's got it; you borrow it, or you can rent it for a couple of dollars. I'm assuming that people have done some research and made sure they're familiar with it. And so I didn't want the first five minutes of this movie to cater to a tiny minority of people who are just going to show up at this, not having seen the first one.

'And it's a very tacky TV kind of device to have, you know... [in a deep voice] "The story of *The Lord of the Rings* so far... " [laughs]. I just approached it like this: my point of view was...people that saw *The Fellowship of the Ring* kind of popped out for a popcorn break that lasted a year [laughs again] and now you're back in on this story and you're just going to roll the next reel. You know, it's going to just rightly carry-on, and I wanted it to have that unity, that kind of feeling.'

144

FILM FACT:

Fran Walsh's voice was used for the Nazgûl scream and sound designer David Farmer provided the Warg howls.

Critics and fans from around the world love *The Lord of the Rings* movies and on Rotten Tomatoes website, they have received an average score of 94 out of a possible 100 per cent. *USA Today* announced in 2007 that *The Lord of the Rings* movies were the most important films of the last 25 years. Will *The Hobbit* be able to top that? We'll have to wait and see.

Tolkien scholars have been less complimentary of the movies, with Wayne G. Hammond writing the following about the first two films: 'I find both of the Jackson films to be travesties as adaptations faithful only on a basic level of plot. Cut and compress as necessary, yes, but don't change or add new material without very good reason. In the moments in which the films succeed, they do so by staying close to what Tolkien so carefully wrote; where they fail, it tends to be where they diverge from him, most seriously in the area of characterisation.

'Most of the characters in the films are mere shadows of those in the book, weak and diminished (notably Frodo) or insulting caricatures (Pippin, Merry, and Gimli).

[T]he filmmakers sacrifice the richness of Tolkien's story and characters, not to mention common sense, for violence, cheap humour, and cheaper thrills. [S]o many of its reviewers have praised it as faithful to the book, or even superior to it, all of which adds insult to injury and is demonstrably wrong.'

To read more about what scholars think of the movies, read the paper: 'The Mines of Moria: Anticipation and Flattening in Peter Jackson's *The Fellowship of the Ring*' by Janet Brennan Croft. A lot of scholars mention the fact that Tolkien himself didn't believe that *The Lord of the Rings* was suitable for 'dramatic representation'.

Peter Jackson's favourite *The Lord of the Rings* movie is *The Return of the King*. He explained why to Steven Head from IGN movies: 'It's climactic. It's got an ending! [laughs]. And it's about time! No, no. It's very, very emotional. And I find it... Aw, well, there's several places where I kind of had tears in my eyes. It's biblical. And it has a kind of climactic sense to it. It's wonderfully over the top and epic. And it's as if at the same time really incredibly emotional, it's a lot about courage. The Frodo/Sam element of the next film is a lot about guts and determination and courage, which I find quite affecting.'

> **FILM FACT:**
>
> The world premiere of *The Return of the King* saw over 100,000 fans attend! It was held at the Embassy Theatre in Wellington, New Zealand.

Peter Jackson likes to have a cameo in all the movies he directs. In the first film he played a drunken citizen of Bree and in the second movie he throws a spear at the Uruk-hai from the top of the gate in the Battle of Helm's Deep. For the third movie he had two cameos. In the first one he was boatswain of a corsair ship and in the second, his hand was used as Sam's hand in the scene where Shelob is wrapping Frodo up. He only did the second cameo because Sean Austin (who plays Sam) wasn't on set and they needed to shoot it so they could move on.

During a live webchat in May 2008, a fan asked Peter: 'Will you have a cameo in this *Hobbit*, and what character would you like to play?' He replied: 'I actually haven't thought about it. My convention is to do cameos in films I direct. I don't know if that extends to films I produce – I guess we'll find out. I love Hobbits! I am a Hobbit, in very many respects, as were my parents. Tolkien wrote about a type of people he knew, in pre-war England, and somewhere along the line, he must have bumped into my relatives!'

SARAH OLIVER

DID YOU KNOW?

Peter Jackson went on a big health kick after filming the third movie because he had tired of being overweight. He lost over 50 pounds (3½ stone). He ditched the fast food and sweets in favour of muesli and yoghurt; he also had laser surgery so he could get rid of his glasses as he was sick of having to clean them when filming on location.

It was important for Peter and the fans that *The Hobbit* movies fitted with *The Lord of the Rings* films and were consistent. At the Sundance Film Festival, Peter told MTV: 'We wanted it to be a part of the five-film series. Fortunately, Tolkien wrote a lot of extra material in the appendices of *The Lord of the Rings*, where he himself kind of tied the two stories together, 20 or 30 years after the publication of *The Hobbit*, so we've been able to use some of that material.'

Master of Lake-town

- Name: Master of Lake-town
- Alias: Old Master, Moneybags, Master of the Lake-men, Master of Esgaroth, Master of the Town
- Race: Men
- Played by: Stephen Fry
- Character description: The Master of Lake-town is greedy and cares for himself over anybody else. When Smaug the dragon attacks, he makes his getaway in his gilded boat.

The actor chosen to play the Master of Lake-town was

Stephen Fry. Stephen is a British actor, born in Hampstead, London. He is also an author, director, playwright, television presenter, poet and journalist. In 2010 he became a director of Norwich City Football Club, the club he has supported since he was a young boy. He is best known for presenting *QI* and playing Peter Kingdom in the TV series, *Kingdom*.

On Thursday, 19 May 2011, director Peter Jackson wrote on his Facebook page to tell fans that Stephen had been cast. He said: 'We are thrilled to confirm that Stephen Fry will be playing The Master of Lake-town. I've known Stephen for several years. In addition to his writing skills, he's a terrific actor and will create a very memorable Master for us.'

DID YOU KNOW?

Stephen Fry has written the screenplay for a remake of the 1955 movie *The Dam Busters*. It is to be directed by Weta designer Christian Rivers and produced by Peter Jackson.

Fry thoroughly enjoyed himself on set and a few months later he told Digital Spy: 'I've done a whole month in New Zealand, in August (which is their winter, oddly enough) and we had a fantastic time. I play this character called the Master of Lake-land, a very gross figure.

'Most of the characters in *The Hobbit* are dwarves, who are wonderfully funny, silvery elfin characters like Orlando, so elegant and beautiful, and there's Bard the Bowman who's handsome and strong. My character is an opportunity for sheer grossness. He's this corrupt mayor, really – the Master of Lake-town, this smelly city on stilts in the lake below the mountain where Smaug the dragon lives. And he [Peter] had me eating testicles, sort of gross appetites. I've got this beard, a bald cap and on top of that a really bad comb-over wig and a wispy moustache and a wispy beard and horrible blotchy skin and disgusting fingernails. And really, really generally speaking an unappetising piece of work and a coward to boot, and very, very greedy.

'We had great fun doing it – the atmosphere on any Peter Jackson set, as any actor will tell you, is wonderful because he's kind and funny and a gentle man. For all his extraordinary power in the business given the success he's had, he's modest, helpful, very easy to work for, and he knows what he wants. And of course he has the most extraordinary technical backup, the Weta Workshop and the Weta Digital, these two things in Wellington that he and Richard Taylor have set up have the best modelling and sculpting and digital facilities in the world – which is why James Cameron went to make *Avatar* there.'

Misty Mountains

Originally, Peter Jackson and his locations team wanted to use Mount Ngauruhoe, North Island as the Misty Mountains that the dwarves and Bilbo go on their quest to find, but they were refused permission. This must have been frustrating as it would have been perfect. Previously, they had used the stratovolcano as Mount Doom in *The Lord of the Rings* movies.

The local Maori Iwi didn't want the shooting to take place because they consider Mount Ngauruhoe and the surrounding mountains as sacred.

Jackson and his team decided instead to use Mount Ruapehu, which is south of Mount Ngauruhoe. Mount Ruapehu is the highest mountain in the North Island. It is still regarded as sacred by the Maori Iwi and they consider it discourteous to photograph the mountain peaks so Peter came to a compromise: they could film the battle on the slopes of one side of the mountain but the peaks would later be added digitally, by using footage from other volcanoes around the world. Happy with this, the tribes of Ngati Rangi and Ngati Uenuku decided to hold a Powhiri, which is a Maori welcoming ceremony with dancing, speeches and singing.

The cast and crew only get one day off a week so no one from the production team expected many of them to visit Maungarongo Marae on their day off. They expected

30 people but 130 turned up, quite remarkable. All the main actors attended because they felt that they should show the Maori Iwi how much they respected them and appreciated being allowed to shoot there. The Ngati Rangi performed a haka, which is their traditional war dance, and then sent a warrior to check out the visitors (this is known as a Tikanga). The cast and crew hadn't been allowed onto the field (called the Marae aitea) but once Zane Weiner (one of the executive producers) took a fern (called a rau and symbolising peace) from the warrior, they were allowed to enter the Marae aitea.

This was extremely moving for all involved and everyone listened intently to the speeches that were then given by representatives from *The Hobbit*, Ngati Rangi and Ngati Uenuku. When it was Sir Ian McKellen's turn to speak, he said: 'You could have easily told Gandalf the Grey "You shall not pass" but you did not.' After each speech there was a song, and when Ian had finished, the dwarves sang the Misty Mountains ballad from the original *Hobbit* book.

Before everyone went their separate ways there was a hongi, which involved the cast and crew getting in line and walking past the Ngati Rangi and Ngati Uenuku people. They had to shake hands, then lean forward so that their foreheads and noses touched their hosts. In doing so, they became tangata whenua (people of the land).

> **DID YOU KNOW?**
>
> While the cast and crew were filming in this location, they had a member of the Maori Iwi with them at all times to watch over them – 'to protect them from the mountain and the mountain from them.' They also had to show their respect by saying 'Good morning, Koro [grandfather]' and 'Good evening, Koro' each day to the mountain.

While shooting on the mountain only essential crew and cast were allowed to be there because lots of endangered moss grows on the mountain slopes. Scaffolding had to be put up to create ramps and runways so that the cast and crew could get about without damaging the moss.

Movement Coach

Everyone wanted to make sure that *The Hobbit* movies were the best they could be, so a movement coach was hired to ensure the hobbits, dwarves, elves and assorted other beings walked in the correct way. The movement coach chosen was Terry Notary, the best in the business.

Terry started out as a stuntman and only became a movement coach by accident, really. In 2000, he was working on the Ron Howard movie *The Grinch*, playing a resident of Whoville. The director wanted all the residents to have the same walk so Terry was given the task of coming up with a walk and a set of movements that the others could follow. Howard admired his work and decided to hire him as the movement coach. This was a completely new role and Terry was the first-ever person to have the title.

Terry went on to work on some huge blockbusters, from *Rise of the Planet of the Apes* to *Transformers: Revenge of the Fallen*, and from *Superman Returns* to *The Incredible Hulk*. He also acts and plays a goblin in *The Hobbit*. In *Planet of the Apes*, he played Rocket and in *Attack the Block*, he was the main alien.

Working on *The Hobbit* was arguably his hardest job to date because there were so many different species. He had to come up with unique movements for each species — how they walked, ran, fought, slept, ate, jumped and then he had to teach the sequences to each actor. Some of them had never played a creature before so it took a while to get their heads around what Terry was asking them to do. Andy Serkis, on the other hand, is just as experienced as Terry and so he didn't require help to play Gollum.

Benedict Cumberbatch enjoyed learning from Terry how he should move when playing Smaug. Back in January 2012, he told a reporter from Collider.com: 'I've already started working out and doing various movement exercises to get myself limber for that all-important jump suit with balls on it, otherwise known as motion-capture.

'It'll be a physical role which I'm no stranger to. I did *Frankenstein* at the beginning of the year with Danny Boyle at the National Theatre and playing the creature in that was a very full-on and sort of corporeal experience.'

Andy Serkis, the actor who plays Gollum, enjoys working with Terry Notary as they are both experts in motion-capture acting. They worked together on *Rise of the Planet of the Apes* as well. Andy hates how people sometimes think that he has only provided the voice of Gollum and the movements for King Kong because what he does is much more than that. The general public don't understand all that motion capture entails and don't see it as acting, even though it is. Without Andy, Gollum wouldn't move the same, as the special effects teams capture Andy's movements first and then build on them to create the Gollum we all know.

DID YOU KNOW?

When Andy Serkis first played Gollum over 10 years ago he had to act in a tin shed, which had seven or so cameras to capture his movements.

New Zealand

Over the last decade, for many of *The Hobbit* and *The Lord of the Rings* cast and crew New Zealand has become a second home. Director Peter Jackson summed it up when he said: 'New Zealand is not a small country but a large village.'

The Christchurch earthquake happened shortly after the majority of the cast had moved to New Zealand and they all remember what it was like. They took part in the two-minute silence held a week after the event, standing in the food tent and reflecting on what had happened. Mark Hadlow (Dori) was particularly affected because

Christchurch means so much to him and as events team leader, he has strong links to the city.

When Ian McKellen (Gandalf) found out that The Isaac Theatre Royal in Christchurch had been temporarily closed because of structural issues and needed big investment if it was to open again, he decided to put on a one-man show to raise funds despite being busy filming *The Hobbit* movies at the time. He had performed *Waiting for Godot* at the theatre just a year before the earthquake struck so felt a personal connection to the theatre. Some of his props survived the earthquake, which Sir Ian felt was quite symbolic.

He told TVNZ: 'I love this beautiful old theatre and want to help restore it as soon as possible. It's only me. No performing dogs, no hobbits. Just Ian McKellen. But the byline is with Tolkien, Shakespeare and you, you being the audience.'

Other events took place to raise money for the theatre, one of them being an online auction, which ran on Trademe from 24 to 30 May 2012. Peter Jackson, Stephen Fry and Mark Hadlow (Dori) all donated items, as did Orlando Bloom, Beyoncé and Dame Maggie Smith. The donations included signed scripts, posters, artwork, DVDs and CDs.

As well as the cast and crew falling in love with New Zealand, Tolkien fans are also doing so because visiting the country is the nearest thing to visiting Middle-earth. When *The Lord of the Rings* came out, tourism received a huge boost so tourism bosses are hoping that *The Hobbit* movies can have just as big an impact this time around.

Chief executive Kevin Bowler told NZ Newswire: 'We are incredibly confident about the future of *The Hobbit* films. We know *The Lord of the Rings* was a great success as a film, but also as an indirect way of promoting New Zealand.'

He also revealed that most of their marketing budget of $65m was to have a *Hobbit* theme. When the DVD/Blu-ray of each of *The Hobbit* movies is released, this will include a promotional clip of New Zealand to try and persuade fans to visit Middle-earth (New Zealand), too.

The main place fans want to visit is Hobbiton, which is located on land belonging to the Alexander family at Haere Mai on the North Island. Before Peter Jackson & Co. arrived, the family had their hands full, looking after the farm's 13,000 sheep and 300 Angus beef cattle, but they now have hundreds of visitors each week wanting to see Bilbo's home.

Peter Jackson first spotted the farm back in September 1998 when he was in a helicopter scouting for possible locations for *The Lord of the Rings*. He thought the farm looked just like Tolkien's descriptions of The Shire and after chatting to the family and bosses from New Line Cinema, a contract was signed. The crew agreed that the unspoilt farmland with a large pine tree in front of a lake was perfect and they set about getting the location ready for filming.

Production designer Dan Hennah recalled in the backstage Production Video 5 how they had found the location: 'We'd been searching pretty much the whole country for this rolling countryside. We were up here scouting around and found this place called Buckland Road and sure enough, when we flew over it we found the round tree, the hill, the lake – it was all meant to be. Of course then it was a matter of talking to the owners of the land, getting their permission to shoot here and build here.'

DID YOU KNOW?

Peter Jackson knocked on the farmhouse door personally to ask for permission to film. It was a Saturday afternoon and the family inside had been busy watching a New Zealand rugby match. The owner of the farm had never heard of *The Lord of the Rings*, although his sons had.

The following March a fleet of trucks, diggers, rollers and bulldozers were brought in by the New Zealand Army and started to build the village. All in all, it took nine months to get it looking just right and to have the roads built. There were 37 hobbit-holes for *The Lord of the Rings*, Hobbiton and the tree overlooking Bag End were bolted together after being chopped up in Matamata and shipped in. Each part of the tree had been numbered so it would look the same as it had done when alive and artificial leaves were added to make it look even more realistic. Back then, the hobbit-holes were made of polystyrene.

The village was only temporary so once the cameras stopped rolling, it was dismantled. This meant that when *The Hobbit* movies got the green light they had to build it all again, but this time around, they wanted permanent buildings to be constructed so that Hobbiton village would be around forever. Work on site started in January 2009 when Guillermo del Toro was the director and back then, filming was expected to begin in 2010. They had no idea of the delays that would put everything back.

DID YOU KNOW?

The Green Dragon was built with a working fireplace and plumbing so it could one day become a real pub.

When director Peter Jackson arrived in Hobbiton on the first day of location shooting he was taken aback. He told the production video cameras: 'Hobbiton is looking fantastic, the art department and the greens department have been working on it for nearly two years. The grasses have grown, the flowers are out – the plastic ones have even bloomed!

'It's weird when you come back to a place you literally thought you would never see again. To be standing there with Elijah dressed up as Frodo, it was the nearest thing I think I'm ever going to come to a time machine.'

If you make the trip to Hobbiton for yourself you will see the streams, bridges and the round front doors to the many hobbit-holes.

FILM FACT

For permanent Hobbiton, there were 44 hobbit-holes built (rather than 37) and each was slightly different from the next. The man in charge of decorating them was Ra Vincent, a sculptor and art director from New Zealand.

The second location that fans love to visit is The Stone Street Studios in Wellington. This is where the green-screen scenes were filmed. Another favourite is the Aratiatia Rapids, where the barrel scenes were shot. There are so many places you can visit in New Zealand which are connected to *The Hobbit* movies and you can choose to explore them on your own or as part of a *Hobbit* tour.

Nori

- Name: Nori
- Alias: None
- Race: Dwarf of the House of Durin
- Played by: Jed Brophy
- Character description: Nori is the middle brother, with Dori as the eldest and Ori as the youngest. He wears a purple hood. Nori isn't afraid to take risks and is not always law abiding. The brothers are distant relations of Thorin and play the flute.

The actor chosen to play Nori was Jed Brophy, a Kiwi actor who has worked with director Peter Jackson many times over the years. Jed got into acting by accident, really. He was studying at an Italian university when he went to see a play called *Wednesday to Come* starring Miranda Harcourt; he loved it so much that he decided to become an actor because it looked like fun. Following this, he did a drama course and then decided to go to drama school. He would later end up playing Ted in another production of *Wednesday to Come* in 2005. The fascinating thing is that Miranda Harcourt was in the production again, playing Ted's sister-in-law Iris.

Jed played Void in comedy–horror movie *Braindead*, John/Nicholas in *Heavenly Creatures* and Snaga and Sharku in *The Lord of the Rings* movies. More recently he has appeared in *King Kong* and *District 9*. When he finished filming *The Lord of the Rings: The Return of the King,* Jed decided to buy the horse that he rode in the movie. A skilled horseman, he enjoys training horses.

Since appearing in *The Lord of the Rings* movies Jed has become a familiar face at *The Lord of the Rings* conventions and enjoys getting to meet the fans (who might not necessarily know who he is because he was heavily disguised in the movies). It used to take six hours for his make-up for Sharku to be applied each day so he would start at 2am and then once he'd finished filming, it would take two hours to remove it all – really hard going because there would be 12 hours of filming on top of the six hours of make-up! At the different conventions around the world, Jed enjoys signing autographs, acting out some scenes and letting fans in on secrets from behind the scenes.

DID YOU KNOW?

Jed's son, Sadwyn Brophy, played Eldarion in *The Lord of the Rings: The Return of the King.* In his spare time Jed writes screenplays and is currently writing one based on a book.

Oin

- Name: Oin
- Alias: None
- Race: Dwarf of the House of Durin
- Played by: John Callen
- Character description: Oin is a dwarf who wears a brown hood. He is the brother of Glóin and they are distant cousins of Thorin.

The actor chosen to play Oin was British actor John Callen. John lived in Blackheath, South London until he was sixteen and then moved to New Zealand with his family. He only stayed in education for one more year before deciding to try art school and then he became a copywriter for a radio station. John loved writing and thought he might have a career in journalism. In his spare time he was acting in an amateur drama group and met someone who thought his voice was perfect for voiceovers.

While recording voiceovers he got to meet some actors and started to record radio plays. Theatre director Mervyn Thompson thought that he had potential and offered him a place in the first professional theatre company in New Zealand. Although thrilled, John continued to write as well, trying his hand at scriptwriting. He began acting in TV shows and 40 years later, he is still working. A talented actor, writer and director, he has performed or directed over 100 plays and 25-plus TV series, and narrated nearly 150 documentaries as well as appearing in several top movies.

Before filming began, John revealed at a press conference: 'When we're together [the dwarf actors], we're a group. We're "as one". But it's not just us – the crew work "as one", too.'

Ori
- Name: Ori
- Alias: None

- Race: Dwarf of the House of Durin
- Played by: Adam Brown
- Character description: Ori is a dwarf who wears a grey hood. He has two older brothers – Dori and Nori – who are also on the quest. They all play the flute.

The actor chosen to play Ori was Adam Brown. In a statement after he was cast, director Peter Jackson told the press: 'Adam is a wonderfully expressive actor and has a unique screen presence. I look forward to seeing him bring Ori to life.'

During a New Zealand press conference, Adam was asked how he got the part. He said: 'I auditioned back in London and kind of got a phone call about four weeks after my audition. I was offered the part from Peter, Fran, Philippa. I was over the moon, really excited about it.'

James Nesbitt joked that Adam got the part because of his versatility and because he was cheap. At this, the other dwarf actors and the journalists present burst into laughter.

Adam Brown is a British actor, comedian and writer. He trained at Middlesex University and has his own comedy theatre company called Plested and Brown with his close friend, Clare Plested. Their website homepage sums up what they are trying to do: 'Our team creates original and innovative new comedy shows that tour the

UK – bringing together irresistible elements of clown, physical comedy and verbal wit.

'Whilst our style of comedy is rooted in the best of British theatrical traditions – self-deprecating, satirical, absurd and fast-moving – our shows have universal appeal. Hence the odd performance in Armenia, New Zealand and South Korea.'

British audiences may recognise Adam from the various TV ads he has done in the past, from Money Supermarket to Virgin, Cheesestrings to Standard Life.

He found being in New Zealand quite surreal, as he remarked in one of Peter's backstage videos: 'What's kind of weird is you're on the sets in the studio and they look so real, you come on location and it almost looks fake. You think, this can't exist – it's just weird, it's a trick. It's mind games.'

Adam had never been in a helicopter before he arrived in New Zealand but he had to get over any initial nerves because they frequently had to use helicopters to get to remote locations.

Peter Jackson

Sir Peter Jackson is a New Zealand movie director, producer and screenwriter. He is best known for directing the three *The Lord of the Rings* movies. Prior to the first *Hobbit* film being released in December 2012, he had won three Oscars personally, 87 other awards and had been nominated for a further 73 during his career. Peter married screenwriter and producer Fran Walsh in 1987 and they went on to have two children, Billy and Katie. Billy was born in 1995 and Katie was born in 1996.

In 2002, Peter was made a Companion of the New Zealand Order of Merit. Eight years later, he was knighted, and in 2012 he received the highest honour possible: the Order of New Zealand in the Queen's Birthday and Diamond Jubilee Honours.

DID YOU KNOW?

Peter likes wearing shorts and wandering around without shoes on when he's filming a movie.

Peter was born on 31 October 1961 and spent his childhood in Pukerua Bay, near Wellington. He was the only son of Bill, a payroll clerk, and factory worker Joan. Both were originally from England and Bill had served in World War II.

As a young boy Peter loved watching *Thunderbirds*. He had lots of Thunderbirds Matchbox toys and he used to think to himself while watching the shows that they were making it up – quite profound for a young child. Even when he was watching movies he would think the same thing – that it was all make-believe. He told film critic David Stratton all about it when asked what compelled him to make films. He said: 'And that sort of was the beginning, really, when I think about it – of, like, the connection of "This isn't real, these are models, you know – they're making all this stuff up". That's what I loved about movies. And that was also fuelled then by seeing the original *King Kong* – the 1933 version of *Kong*, which I saw when I was nine. And I remember that weekend I made plasticine dinosaurs and started to try to do some stop-motion animation with my little Super-8 camera. For a lot of my childhood, I didn't want to direct movies because I didn't really know what directing was, but I wanted to do special effects. And everything was, you know, really playing with special effects. And then I wanted my special effects movies to have little stories and plots. And so the concept of writing and directing was something that very slowly sort of grew on me, almost without me knowing.'

Watching the first *Batman* movie was a significant moment in Peter's life and he can still remember how it felt today. He revealed to *Esquire* magazine: 'One of the first movies I ever saw was *Batman*, based on the TV series with Adam West and Burt Ward. They had this fireman's pole. They'd jump on this pole in civilian clothes, and as they arrived at the bottom, they were in their Batman and Robin costumes. I was only four or five years old at the time, and I was amazed by this magical transformation. I remember asking my older cousin, "How do they do that?" My cousin must've been about eight, and he said, "Oh, that's just special effects." I can still remember hearing those words for the first time. In some respects, I can chart everything I've ever done since back to that moment.'

Some reports suggest that Peter was given his Super-8 camera by a family friend; others say that his parents bought it for Christmas 1969 to record weekend breaks, but whatever happened, Peter got his hands on a camera and started making his own movies with friends. At the age of twelve he made his own version of *King Kong*, a movie he would end up writing, directing and producing for release in 2005. He revealed: '*Kong* is my most long-term unfinished project because I started making my version of *King Kong* when I was about 12 years old. I made a little puppet and a cardboard model of the Empire State Building and I had my little King Kong and I did some stop motion. And I abandoned the film pretty quickly – I realised at the age of 12 that doing a remake of *King Kong* was a little ambitious.'

Throughout his teens, he filmed hundreds of short films with friends, including *Revenge of the Gravewalker*, *The Dwarf Patrol* and *Coldfinger*, a James Bond spoof. He would do his own special effects on a shoestring budget. Fascinated with World War I, he dug a hole in his parents' back garden to build trenches for war films. All he wanted to do was make movies and so he left college and got a job that would give him enough money to carry on filmmaking.

Peter worked as a photolithographer at the *Evening Post* newspaper, Wellington, but outside of work carried on making his own films. When he was 22 he began work on a comedy about aliens called *Bad Taste*. While editing the movie he met Fran Walsh, the screenwriter and producer who was to become his wife. Former marketing director of New Zealand's Film Commission, Lindsay Shelton recalled how she first met Peter to the *Observer*: 'In the 1980s a series of *Worzel Gummidge* was shot in New Zealand. One of the writers was Fran Walsh. One day during shooting she asked if she could bring a friend because he wanted to get into making films. That friend's name was Peter Jackson. He took a lowly part in the crew and appeared in one episode as a farmer.'

It took Peter four years to make *Bad Taste* but it was well worth the effort when it was shown at the Cannes Film Festival and became a cult classic. He quit his job and started writing, producing and directing other splatstick movies such as *Meet the Feebles* (1989) and *Braindead* (1992). In a 2010 interview with the *Telegraph* he said of his splatstick movies: 'To me, they were a joke. We enjoyed being crazy and anarchic and upsetting the people we wanted to upset in those days.'

After various splatstick movies he wrote, produced and directed *Heavenly Creatures*, which was released in 1994. It was his first mainstream movie and starred an unknown Kate Winslet and Melanie Lynskey. It was actually his wife Fran who suggested they do a movie on the famous

Parker-Hulme murder case because it had gripped New Zealand for over 40 years. At the Toronto Film Festival, Peter confided in film critic Emanuel Levy: 'I immediately fell in love with this unusual tale – I actually became obsessed with it. The relationship [between the girls] was for the most part a rich and rewarding one, and we tried to honour that in our film. Our intention was to make a film about an intense relationship that went terribly wrong.'

Kate Winslet says of her first movie: '[It was] an incredible experience. I just loved it. But it was also really traumatising – true story, lots of harrowing scenes.'

After *Heavenly Creatures*, Peter filmed a TV mockumentary called *Forgotten Silver* (1995) before filming his first big budget movie, *The Frighteners* (released in 1996). Despite the movie being set in North America it was filmed in New Zealand at his request, with Weta Workshop doing the special effects. The movie starred Michael J. Fox as Frank Bannister. On release, *The Frighteners* underperformed – perhaps due to competition from the *Independence Day* movie starring Will Smith and the fact that the Atlanta Olympics started the very same day. Peter told the studio about the clash because it might have prevented audiences from heading to the cinema but they replied: 'We don't think so; our research indicates that's not the case.'

'And I just thought how the hell do they know? There

had only ever been three Olympic Games held in the United States in 100 years!'

Peter's next movie was supposed to be *King Kong* but Universal Studios put it on hold because other similar movies – *Godzilla* and *Mighty Joe Young* – were already in production. At the time he was very disappointed because it was a movie he was desperate to make but looking back, he's so glad he didn't get to make it then. He explained to Contact Music: 'It was the blackest day of my career when Universal cancelled the previous one, but now I'm grateful because it worked out for the best. We wouldn't have done such a good job on *Kong* back then and now we are able to apply everything we learned from *The Lord of the Rings*.'

He then went on to write, produce and direct the three *The Lord of the Rings* movies, which were all huge box-office hits (see also *The Lord of the Rings* section of this book). Peter finally got to film *King Kong* and it was released on 14 December 2005. It was a box-office success, taking $550 million worldwide. Naomi Watts (who played actress Ann Darrow) admitted in an interview with About.com: 'I don't think I could have just signed on to this project had it not have been [for] someone like Peter. I would have been concerned that it would have just been too much of an action movie and a damsel in distress. But when I first heard about it, and I heard that Peter was doing it, I thought, wow, that's interesting! The guy who is pretty much the front runner in terms of the effects world, as well as the man who made *Heavenly Creatures*, which is a beautifully complicated movie about very emotional stuff. So it seemed like a great idea. Then I went and met with him and his partner Fran Walsh and Philippa Boyens, their writing partner. I heard them speak about it, that it was the legendary *King Kong* but with a number of great new ideas and how they definitely wanted to change the female role into something much more than just a screaming beauty.'

Peter's next big movie was *The Lovely Bones* (released on 11 December 2009). He had to credit Fran and Philippa with introducing him to the Alice Sebold novel, *The Lovely Bones*, in 2002, which led to him wanting to do a movie adaptation. He had been in London doing the score for *The Lord of the Rings: The Two Towers* when Philippa flew over to see him from New Zealand. She had bought the novel in an airport bookstore and passed it on to Fran to read once she'd finished it. Both were blown away by the story so Peter decided to read it for himself. He explained to journalist Stuart Husband: 'We were getting to the age where we were starting to lose friends and relations [Peter's parents died while he was filming *The Lord of the Rings*] and the book speaks to all those things, plus it's kind of comforting, too.

'But I can honestly say that adapting *The Lovely Bones* was the hardest thing we've ever done. The book is like a wonderful puzzle and you have to make decisions about what to leave in or take out.'

Indeed he was criticised by some fans of the book because he didn't show the murder or the attack, but he argues: 'It's a film about how love never really dies and how time heals. It's not a murder film and I wanted kids to be able to go and see it. Film is such a powerful medium. It's like a weapon and I think you have a duty to self-censor.'

He explained further in an interview with Orange: 'We feel that the movie is a positive movie for young kids to see. We have a daughter who's 12 and we've shown her the film and she said: "Dad, if it was me I would have gone down there with Mr Harvey [the murderer], too!" So, she is already thinking about if she found herself in that particular circumstance. I think it's good that that particular aspect of things can be portrayed in a way. And, ultimately, we wanted to have the film to feel sort of positive, too – that was very important for us.'

In 2009, Jackson produced *District 9*, which directed by Niall Bomkamp. A surprise hit, it was eventually nominated for four Oscars. Speaking to the *Los Angeles Times* at ComicCon that year, Peter said: 'I think one of the good things with that movie is that no one is expecting anything, really. So I think one of the advantages we've had is we've sort of come out as a complete surprise, which was actually quite good, really. It wasn't really planned that way but we quietly made it down to South Africa and New Zealand, sort of under the radar. It was never a film that people knew about until it suddenly started getting the trailers and the posters started going around.'

For Jackson's next movie – *The Adventures of Tintin* – he was the producer, with Steven Spielberg directing. He did, however, film some of the scenes before filming for *The Hobbit* began and worked with Weta Digital in post-production. It was a big hit worldwide, taking $373 million at the box office, and a sequel was planned for 2013. For *The Adventures of Tintin: Red Rackham's Treasure* their roles would be reversed; it would be Spielberg producing and Jackson directing.

While promoting the first movie Peter told journalist Rebecca Murray: 'I find that in the process of making a film you're constantly discovering things that you never even imagined would work at the beginning. When I start a film, you know I can sort of shut my eyes, sit somewhere quiet and imagine the movie finished. I can imagine the camera angles; I can even imagine the type of music. Without knowing the tune, I can imagine the type of music it needs to be. But in the process of making the film, you're constantly discovering new things all of the time. I mean, actors come into the film and do things you never even imagined. Production designers come in, the director of photography lights it in a way that you never imagined. So, it's always evolving, always exciting.'

In October 2011, Peter was asked by the New Zealand Prime Minister which of his own movies he liked the best. He couldn't decide and said: 'Oh, I don't know, I mean it's difficult – I never watch my movies, that's the problem. I literally never look at them after I've finished them. Occasionally if I'm somewhere in a hotel and I flick around the channels and I find one of my films on, I kind of watch it for two or three minutes just out of interest [laughs] and then all the memories start coming back and I change the channel. So I don't know – I must admit I've got a real yearning to watch *Meet The Feebles* again. I haven't seen *Meet the Feebles*, which we made in about 1989 – I haven't seen that almost for 15 years, I guess now – 15/16 years, so I wouldn't mind seeing that again. I don't know if it's my favourite, so I'll have to wait and see.'

Picking his favourite movies by other people is much easier, and Peter would say his favourites are the original 1933 *King Kong* and the 1926 silent movie classic, *The General*.

Peter adores his two children, Katie and Billy. When Katie was thirteen she used to spend her weekends making her own movies with her friends, following in his footsteps. She would edit them on iMovie and show her father what she had done. However, she must have grown out of it as Peter admitted during an interview with the *Telegraph*, back in January 2010: 'My kids send up what I do mercilessly, which is a very healthy thing, I don't think either of them want to be film-makers, probably because they've spent their formative years getting excruciatingly bored on movie sets.

'I've got some credit from my son for *The Lovely Bones*, but only because we've got Michael Imperioli and he's just worked his way through *The Sopranos* box set. Other than that, they're not terribly impressed.'

Back in 2001, both children had a small cameo in *The Lord of the Rings: The Fellowship of the Ring* in a scene at the Prancing Pony. Peter had planned for them to be in a scene with Gandalf showing them a magic trick at Bilbo's birthday party but it ended up being cut. Katie has also appeared in the other two *The Lord of the Rings* movies, *King Kong* and *The Lovely Bones*. She played a hobbit in *The Hobbit* movies – can you spot her?

Billy, being the eldest child, started acting in Peter's movies earlier; he played a baby in a bouncer in the 1996 horror movie *The Frighteners*. He also had cameos in *The Lord of the Rings* movies, *King Kong* and *The Lovely Bones* but has since decided that he doesn't really want to be an actor and so he wasn't after a part in *The Hobbit*. He is sixteen now and goes to Scots College, Wellington. His school did a fund-raiser for victims of the Christchurch earthquake, attended by Sir Ian McKellen. He has known the family for over a decade so they are all pretty close. When *The Lord of the Rings* filming wrapped, Peter and Fran presented him with a special book containing 100 photos of people involved in the movies. They were taken informally, just like a family photo album.

Peter only became the director of *The Hobbit* movies in October 2010 after Guillermo del Toro stepped down. In the days when he was executive producer and Guillermo was the director, fans asked Peter if he could clarify what his role involved. He said: 'Truth is "executive producers" do a range of things on movies, from a lot to virtually nothing! I see myself being one of a production team; my interest is helping Guillermo make the very best films he can. I love writing and I'm looking forward to that. Guillermo will be writing, along with Fran, Philippa and myself. As a director, I could never direct something I didn't have a hand in writing, and we're not expecting Guillermo to do that either. If the director is part of the writing, it means he was there when the discussions took place, story decisions were made; he knows why things are the way they are, and what they need to achieve. Everything is in a script for a reason and only by being part of a writing team (or writing it yourself) do you really understand the intention of every beat.

'I see my role as being part of that writing team, which will create the blueprint and then helping Guillermo construct the movie. I want Guillermo to make his movies and I want to make sure we end up with a five-movie series that's as good as it can possibly be.'

Shortly before filming was due to start, Peter was rushed to hospital. The next day, *The Hobbit* publicist released the following statement: 'Sir Peter Jackson was admitted to Wellington Hospital on Wednesday night with acute stomach pains. He subsequently underwent surgery for a perforated ulcer. Sir Peter is currently resting comfortably and his doctors expect him to make a full recovery. Sir Peter's surgery is not expected to impact on his directing commitment to *The Hobbit* beyond a slight delay to the start of filming.'

Ian McKellen was very surprised at how well Peter looked when he saw him after surgery. He wrote on his blog: 'For someone recovering from major abdominal surgery, Peter is looking better than fine, though it's still a surprise to see a slim-line rather than cherubic PJ, remembering first time round when there was always a tempting bowl of sweets ("candy" to the Americans and "lollies" to the Kiwis) by the director's chair. His eyes seem darker, more pronounced, more purposeful. He showed me his scar and said he is raring to go.'

In an interview, John Rhys-Davies (who played Gimli in *The Lord of the Rings* movies) joked that he felt that he was to blame for Peter's stomach ulcer because he had offered to appear in *The Hobbit* movies after initially refusing. He told stuff.co.nz: 'The other day, when I realised it was about to start, a little shiver of regret went through me. So I called Peter Jackson's assistant and said, "If there was anything or even just an excuse to come down, do let me know." PJ promptly collapsed and was admitted to hospital. I never heard back – I didn't think I was that bad!'

The members of the cast who had never worked with Peter before didn't know exactly what to expect but they understood when they saw how so many actors and crewmembers work with him time and again – he's such a nice guy. Martin Freeman revealed to New Zealand journalists: 'For somebody who is as rich as Croesus and has that many Oscars, he's phenomenally normal. And I mean genuinely normal, as opposed to those people that play at being hip or cool or ostentatiously normal – sort of "look here's me being normal and having a normal cup of tea." No, PJ is a practitioner, not a star. I get the feeling that if you were to have known him when he was twelve, he's basically the same person now – an enthusiast.'

James Nesbitt (Bofur) talked about Peter, Fran and Philippa, saying: 'They're great listeners and take on board what you have to offer.'

DID YOU KNOW?

Peter used to tell *The Hobbit* extras in the Hobbiton scenes to have a laugh and a joke during breaks in filming because he wanted them to be happy and jolly all the time.

On Peter's 50th birthday the dwarves surprised him with a special calendar featuring a different dwarf in a sexy pose for each month. Sadly the calendar hasn't been made available for fans to see or buy.

In his spare time Peter likes to paint toy soldiers and make model airplanes, something he has enjoyed doing since he was a young boy. He had a great time on the Easter four-day holiday from shooting *The Hobbit* movies. On Wednesday, 4 May 2011 Peter told fans what he got up to on his Facebook page: 'A pic from Easter. We went down to the Omaka airshow, and I got to fulfill one of my childhood dreams to sit in the cockpit of a Spitfire. Thank you, Brendon and Sean.

'The Supermarine Spitfire is the single greatest aircraft ever, hands down, no debate. We should all be grateful the British government decided to put an order in for several hundred, back in 1936. The events of the summer of 1940 may have had a different ending otherwise. Is there anything else designed over 70 years ago that remains as beautiful, powerful, potent and just all-round cool as this aircraft? My second childhood dream is to fly one. I don't know, maybe one day. But not until we get these movies finished!'

Props

The costumes for *The Hobbit* movies were designed by Ann Maskrey and Richard Taylor; Richard also had to supervise Weta Workshop, who were making the weapons, armour, props and prosthetics. He had to tell them exactly which designs he wanted them to make.

Props from *The Hobbit* and *The Lord of the Rings* movies are extremely valuable and if sold can go for huge amounts of money. One of the jewellers who made props for *The Hobbit* and *The Lord of the Rings* movies was distraught when burglars broke into his home in Paraparaumu, New Zealand on 4 May 2011.

The burglars stole everything of value they could from Dallas Poll, including hard drives containing over 25,000 family photographs, his computer, TV, guitars and priceless props that he will never be able to replace. They stole his *Star Wars* Stormtrooper costume, which he wore to events to raise money for children's charities and a replica sword that he was given after acting as Aragorn's double in *The Lord of the Rings* movies. Other items that were stolen included a *King Kong* Venatosaurus Bust and a highly collectable *The Lord of the Rings* statue of Sam Gamgee and Bill the Pony.

Poll told Stuff.co.nz: 'It is devastating. They took sentimental items – a lot of personal stuff I really want back.

'[Talking about the sword] It is a concern it has got into the wrong hands – it is still a large steel sword.'

Tolkien fans tried to help by keeping an eye out in case any of the items appeared for sale in chatrooms or on selling sites but so far nothing has appeared and the police are still investigating.

Fiona Thomson from Glenview, New Zealand was one of the team who had to create the clothing and armour for Martin Freeman and the actors who play the dwarves and the goblins. She normally runs a cobbler's shop but spent four months on *The Hobbit* set. Usually she spends her time working with leather to make bags, wallets and belts, so creating armour was something out of the ordinary for her. She wasn't daunted, though, because she has over 30 years' experience. Once she'd finished and returned home, she kept her lips sealed because she was sworn to secrecy and didn't want anyone finding out the armour designs before the first movie was in cinemas.

The prop everybody was looking forward to seeing was Thorin's sword: the Orcrist. In *The Hobbit* book, the sword was crafted by elves and glows blue whenever there are goblins or orcs nearby. Richard Armitage was probably the most excited about seeing it for the first time because he would be the one wielding it. He thought it looked beautiful but was surprised how heavy it was when he picked it up. The rest of the dwarf actors were thrilled when they saw the armour they would be wearing after Smaug's death – it was even better than they'd imagined.

During filming the cast and crew got the bad news that Bob Anderson had died at the age of 89. Over the years, he had been a sword-master/trainer for many blockbusters, including *The Lord of the Rings*, *Star Wars*, *Pirates of the Caribbean* and *The Legend of Zorro*.

Once he learned the sad news, Peter Jackson wrote on his Facebook page: 'It is rare, even within the film industry, that you get to work with a legend which was why I was thrilled when Bob Anderson agreed to come on board *The Lord of the Rings* as our sword-master. In fact, it took a while for it to sink in that I was going to get to work with the same man who had helped create some of cinema's greatest fight sequences – from *Star Wars* to *The Princess Bride*. Bob was a brilliant swordsman and a gifted teacher; I will remember him as a wonderfully

SARAH OLIVER

patient man, possessed of a terrific sense of humour. It was a privilege to have known him.'

The crew and cast were also saddened to learn that David Bain, a master cooper who had made the barrels that the dwarves escape in, had died before shooting finished. David was originally from Scotland, where he learnt his craft before immigrating to New Zealand after meeting his wife. He had worked as a cooper on *The Lord of the Rings* movies, *The Chronicles of Narnia: The Witch and The Wardrobe*, *Underworld* and finally, *The Hobbit*.

David shared his name with a New Zealand murderer and people would often bring it up in conversation but he didn't let it bother him, saying instead: 'It was my name long before it was his.' He had been diagnosed with an inoperable brain tumor on 24 February 2012 and died on 26 April, a few days before his daughter's wedding. His wife Maureen told Stuff.co.nz: 'We will be having two celebrations this week; one of David's life at his funeral tomorrow and one for the start of our daughter's new life.

'[He was] everything to all people. He could be serious, funny, infuriating even. He was full of surprises. We'd been married nearly 30 years and he would always come out with something unexpected.

'He was cheated of a couple of decades or so, but what he managed to pack into [his life] was amazing.'

Prosthetics

In order for the movie Bilbo to have furry feet just like the Bilbo in the book, Heather McMullen was hired to create the hobbit feet for Martin Freeman and the other hobbits to wear. Heather is a make-up, hair and prosthetics artist who trained at Madame Tussauds London. She has worked in the theatre making wigs, created eyebrows for the goblins in Gringotts on the final *Harry Potter* movie and did the make-up for the cast of *The Lion King Musical*. In addition, she has a lot of experience in trauma make-up, making actors look like they are dead for TV shows and plays.

After she got the job of *The Hobbit* feet, Heather had to relocate to New Zealand so she could be close by while they were filming. She spent hours every day getting the feet ready; each piece of silicone skin needed lots of human hair to be attached to it so it looked right. It was a painstaking process. Heather wanted to make sure that each one was perfect before Martin put it on. While he was filming she would be watching just to check that the feet remained intact. If they were damaged, maybe some hair fell off or a toe got ripped, she would go to Martin as soon as the scene finished and would swap them for an identical pair of feet. The director and crew were far too busy to look out for damage to Martin's feet so the pressure was all on her.

If short of time she could get a new pair of feet ready in just over an hour and a half but she liked to spend much longer when time was available.

The feet in *The Hobbit* movies were a lot more advanced than those used in *The Lord of the Rings* movies. Back then the feet were glued on each day and were like shoes. For *The Hobbit*, the feet were actually made of silicone skin and went all the way up the actor's legs and stopped just over the knees. Martin Freeman and some of the more important hobbits had advanced hobbit feet, which allowed them to twitch their toes – something that couldn't be done with standard hobbit feet.

Each day Heather and the make-up team had to help *The Hobbit* actors put on their feet before filming started and take them off once filming was over. By the end of the day they would be filled with sweat – yuck! On days when they were filming in Hobbiton there were 70 sets to take off, which made it rather time consuming.

FILM FACT:

Three people worked in the 'Flesh Factory' and made the dwarves' fat suits.

The make-up and prosthetics teams had to approach the way they worked carefully, as prosthetics supervisor Tami Lane explained in the 4th production video: '3D, 48 frames is pretty unforgiving and we had to change our whole way of going about colouring these things because what we found out in early tests was if there wasn't enough red in these pieces they would punch up yellow and react differently than normal skin with blood running through it.'

Some of the actors (those playing dwarves and Gandalf), who would be needing beards and moustaches in the movies, had not shaved for quite a few weeks when they arrived on set but they were all told they had to be clean-shaven before filming started. This was to ensure that the fake beards and moustaches would stick on correctly with spirit gum. They also had to wear wigs and the hobbit actors needed to wear hobbit ears.

The man in charge of the transformation was Rick Findlater, key make-up and hair supervisor on *The Hobbit* movies. Ian McKellen, Elijah Wood and Cate Blanchett knew him well because he had been a hair and make-up stylist on *The Lord of the Rings* movies. Rick is a fast worker and doesn't waste any time. To get a wig, beard and moustache on a dwarf actor takes him only an hour but with so many to do, it's just as well he has other make-up and hair stylists to help him, otherwise it would take all day to get them ready. Some of the actors had to wear fake noses and other prosthetics, too.

On his blog, Sir Ian McKellen discussed the first time

that Rick turned him into Gandalf for *The Hobbit* movies. He recalled: 'The false nose too looked not quite as we'd remembered. That's because it wasn't. I had requested a smaller nose than last time. The WETA sculptors were making new noses anyway, silicone replacing the old sticky gelatine, which tended to slide around if the wizard sneezed or shouted.

'It's like old times. Gandy's clothes are hanging round my trailer and in steps Emma Harre, who dressed me last time, valiant, sporting, reliable and ready to put up once more with my early morning grumps and end-of-day sloth. We giggle as we remember the tricks of the layered costume, the hidden belts and braces. It's all new, and looking it, and will till broken down. But it fits, even the new hat. I stride over to the Studio smiling.'

DID YOU KNOW?

Sir Ian was banned from wearing his Gandalf costume from *The Lord of the Rings*. He explained in his blog: 'The original costume I wore in *LOTR* hangs rather mournfully on a stand by the camera. I can't wear it in *The Hobbit*, because it has been noted "of historic status". Ann has made two changes, which few may notice but please me because they revert to Tolkien's introduction in *Fellowship of the Ring*, where he mentions a silver scarf and black boots.

'In the film, a scarf appeared just once, tied to Gandalf's cart at Hobbiton but oddly not thereafter. I now have a substantial, magic-looking silvery scarf to wear and act with and perhaps find some part of its own to play. I've already twisted it into a stylish turban. And, as per JRR Tolkien, below the familiar gown, a new pair of black boots may be spied. They will not look new, of course. They are riding boots, the sort that can be pulled on in a hurry. Gandalf is often in a hurry. His previous boots were laced and needed Emma to get on and off. Not good for a wizard on the run. And they were grey, not black.'

Richard Armitage had never been in a role that required as much make-up as playing Thorin did. He confessed to Kevin P. Sullivan from MTV: 'We all started with quite an extreme version of ourselves. I think because my character does spend a lot of time onscreen and you really have to understand what he's going through emotionally, it became clear that if we started to make the prosthetic as close to my features as possible but still make him a dwarf, it would be much easier to read the character. He has to go on such a journey, it was really important to do that. I grew my own beard after the first block because I felt that it was restricting my face. The jaw is so connected to emotion that I wanted to have that free. It made such a huge difference.

'It's really weird now because I can't play the character when I haven't gotten everything on. It's very hard to rehearse when you're not in costume, when you haven't gotten the prosthetics on, but I look in the mirror when it's all finished and I don't see it. I can't see where it starts and where it ends; I just see the character – I've never had that before. It's such a unique experience. It's a face that doesn't belong to me – it belongs to WETA workshop and the people that created it.'

Quitting with regret

Guillermo del Toro was the original director of *The Hobbit* movies but he quit before filming began. He wrote the script alongside Peter Jackson (who replaced him as director), Philippa Boyens and Fran Walsh.

Guillermo is a Mexican director, producer, screenwriter and designer. He is best known for his movies *Pan's Labyrinth*, *Blade II* and the *Hellboy* series. Born in Guadalajara, Jalisco, Mexico, he had a troubled childhood, confessing to the *Guardian* in 2006: 'I have said sometimes that I have spent 32 years recuperating from my first 10 years. Really. I had a pretty screwed-up childhood, living in Mexico.'

As a young boy, Guillermo started filming his own movies, using a Super-8 camera like Peter Jackson did. He trained at the Centro de Investigación y Estudios Cinematográficos in Guadalajara. He learnt all about make-up for movies and special effects from Dick Smith, the legendary Oscar winning make-up artist, and started his career as a special effects make-up designer.

The first movie that he worked on as a director was *Cronos*, which was released in 1993. While filming his second movie (*Mimic*), his father was kidnapped in Mexico and Guillermo had to pay a huge ransom to get him released, twice what the kidnappers had originally asked for. After this he and his family had to leave Mexico for good as there was always the threat that kidnappers could target them again.

Though viewed by many people as a fantasy and horror director, Guillermo has directed many different types of movies over the years. One of his earliest memories is when he was two years old and thought he saw green ants walking up his wall after watching an episode of *Outer Limits*. He also thought there were monsters in his bedroom and once famously said to one of these imaginary monsters: 'If you're nice to me and let me get up and go to the bathroom, I'll devote my life to you.' Guillermo made it to the bathroom and began making horror movies when he was old enough!

He stepped down as *The Hobbit* director because he was concerned about scheduling. Since May 2010, he has produced *Biutiful*, *Julia's Eyes*, *Don't Be Afraid of the Dark*, *Kung Fu Panda 2*, *Puss in Boots*, *The Captured Bird*, *Mama*, *Rise of the Guardians*, *The Incredible Hulk* TV series, directed *Pacific Rim* and *Pinocchio* and has been the creative consultant for *Megamind*!

DID YOU KNOW?

Guillermo del Toro and Peter Jackson first met at a *The Lord of the Rings* party at Bob Shaye's house. Del Toro likes to joke that they polished off a tray of shrimp and discussed how New Line 'should keep hiring round, bearded directors with funny accents!' Back then, they had no idea that they would be working on *The Hobbit* together.

Guillermo said yes to directing *The Hobbit* because he had loved the book as a child and actually planned on including a dragon very much like Smaug in his movie *Pan's Labyrinth* until budget restrictions stopped him. He admitted to fans during an online webchat: 'When I saw Peter undertake the Trilogy I thought that *The Hobbit* would never come to be for me. The proposition of spending half a decade crafting these films received – as Peter will attest – a five-second "YES" from me. To people in my industry I'm usually a guy that tries to generate his own projects and I remain very elusive when people try and attach me to big projects. For decades I have passed on films of enormous scope but this is a fantastic privilege and I immediately said "Yes".'

In the same webchat Peter was asked what it was about Guillermo that made him the right person for the job. He responded: 'Watching his films, he has respect for fantasy – he understands it, he's not frightened by it. Guillermo also understands character, and how the power of any movie is almost always linked to how closely we empathise with characters within the story. His work shows great care and love for the main characters he creates. He also has supreme confidence with design, and visual effects. So many filmmakers are scared of visual effects, which is no crime but tough if you're doing one of these movies!

'If we disagree, the director has to win because you should never force a director to shoot something they don't believe in. But we're both reasonably practical and ego-free, and I believe that if we disagree, we both have the ability to express our differing theories – state our case, like lawyers – and between us, work out what's best for the movie.'

Guillermo had first read *The Hobbit* as a child but he hadn't read any of the other Tolkien books until he signed up for directing *The Hobbit*. During a post on

TheOneRing.net forum, he admitted: 'At the age of 11 I read *The Hobbit* and it enchanted me as only a classic Fairy-Tale can – it had enough darkness and dread and emotion to make a profound impression that lasted [with] me until now. Beorn, Mirkwood, the Wargs, Smaug, the Riddles in the Dark, they have all lived with me for many years.

'Nevertheless at that early age, the rest of Tolkien proved to contain Geography and Genealogy too complex for my prepubescent brain.

'And here I am now: reading like a madman to catch up with a whole new land, a continent of sorts – a Cosmology created by [a] brilliant philologist turned Shaman.'

Guillermo was actually inspired by *The Hobbit* when writing and directing his 2006 movie, *Pan's Labyrinth*. He confessed: 'In creating *Pan's Labyrinth*, I drank deep of the most rigid form of Fairy Lore and tried to contextualise the main recurrent motifs in an instinctive rhyme between the world of fantasy and the delusions of War and Politics (the grown man's way of playing make-believe) and in re-reading *The Hobbit* just recently I was quite moved by discovering, through Bilbo's eyes the illusory nature of possession, the sins of hoarding and the banality of war – whether in the Western Front or at a Valley in Middle-earth. Lonely is the mountain indeed.'

In another post on TheOneRing.net forum, he confessed: 'My calculator has been in pretty bad shape since my very first movie. With the exception of *Devil's Backbone*, I have always deferred part or the total of my salary when making a film. And after the kidnapping of my father in the late 1990s after being on the brink of bankruptcy, I still turned down *Narnia* and the third *Harry Potter* film. I don't need to bend to make a living otherwise I would do *Pan's* or *DBB* in between big movies.'

He and Peter Jackson complemented each other and certainly didn't have any major bust-ups while working together on *The Hobbit*. They did quarrel at times over certain things and sometimes Guillermo would win; at other times it would be Peter's turn. Guillermo summed up how much he respects his fellow director in an interview with DigitalActing.com. He said: 'Two filmmakers have produced me in my life, both named Peter. One was Pedro Almodóvar and one is Peter Jackson. Both times my experience has been that they are perfect producers because they understand the producer is not a producer/director.

'A producer is a producer. If there's an emergency, if everything goes wrong, then the producer can – and should – have a strong opinion. But while everything is going well, on time, on budget and is creatively solid, there's no need for that.'

When del Toro stepped down he felt that Peter Jackson should be the one to take over as director because the director needed to be someone who lived and breathed all they had done over the past two years. The new director must completely understand the script and the vision so Peter was the obvious choice. Guillermo did feel, however, that if Peter did take the job he would redesign Smaug, which must have been hard because he had been so passionate about the design.

When asked how hard it was to quit during a BBC *Film 2010* interview, Guillermo said: 'It doesn't get harder than that – it was the hardest decision I've ever taken. I have incredible heartache, I feel terrible about it. It's very hard, it's getting a little easier to talk about it but essentially, it's like you've been recently widowed and everybody asking you exactly how your wife died. It's pretty morbid.

'There was no other choice. I kept postponing, I kept fending off the problems, I kept compartmentalising. We did everything we could with *The Hobbit* – I feel like the guy in the real-life experience that Danny Boyle just did his movie. I was hanging by a thread of my arm for so long that at the end of the day, you had to cut it off. Do I like having one arm less? No. But did I have to? Yes.'

He also revealed that he would go and see *The Hobbit* movies when they come out, and that he would probably like them.

Radagast

- Name: Radagast
- Alias: Aiwendil ('Friend of Birds'), Radagast the Simple, Radagast the Fool, Radagast the Brown, Radagast the Bird-tamer
- Race: Maiar/Istari/Ithryn
- Played by: Sylvester McCoy
- Character description: Gandalf says he is his cousin, but that could mean they just have a strong friendship. He is a friend of Beorn and wears brown robes.

The actor chosen to play Radagast was Sylvester McCoy

(his non-stage name is Percy James Patrick Kent-Smith). Sylvester is a Scottish actor, born in Dunoon, Strathclyde. His parents were both Irish but lived in Scotland. Sylvester's father died in World War II before he was born and so he was brought up by his mum, nan and aunties.

At school he couldn't decide what he wanted to be when he grew up but eventually settled on becoming a priest, attending a seminary in Aberdeen from the age of twelve to sixteen. At Blairs College seminary he studied hard and became keen on history; he also became a fan of classical music. On reaching sixteen, he decided that he would rather become a monk than a priest, but when he applied he was told that he was too young. This rejection altered the course of his life because he had to go to Dunoon Grammar School instead and while there, he got to mix with girls on a daily basis. He decided he liked girls too much to become a monk and so after finishing school he moved to London and got a job at an insurance company. He stayed with the company until he was twenty-seven and then got a job in the box office of the Roundhouse Theatre.

He confided in Sheila Connor from *The British Theatre Guide*: 'The Roundhouse in the sixties and seventies was a wonderful place where lots of avant-garde plays were put on, and lots of rock concerts. I was a bouncer for the Rolling Stones one night. I got a job there because it was a real swinging sixties hippy place – and I knew the cook! By then I'd dropped out of the City and grew my hair long. I just didn't want to be in the City life and they said they wanted a hippy for accounts.'

He became an actor by accident really, he explains: 'Brian Murphy (the actor most famous for playing George Roper in the ITV sitcom *Man About the House*) used to collect the tickets I sold because his wife was an administrator at the Roundhouse, so when he wasn't working he'd collect tickets, and he just thought I was an actor and he recommended me to a guy called Ken Campbell, so it was all by accident that I joined.'

He joined the Ken Campbell Roadshow theatre group with Bob Hoskins, Dave Hill, Jane Wood and a few others. The group would perform in pubs and pretty much any venue going. One night, they were booked to appear at a circus so their director decided to create a circus act with a stuntman called Sylvester McCoy. The play's programme noted that the part of Sylvester McCoy was played by an actor called Sylvester McCoy, but it was actually being played by Percy. Although the director meant this to be a joke, one critic thought there really was a guy called Sylvester McCoy. When he realised this, Percy decided to adopt the name Sylvester McCoy as his stage name.

During his time with the Ken Campbell Roadshow he came to the attention of a director called Joan

Littlewood and was encouraged to audition for several plays. He became a very successful stage actor before landing his big break in TV by becoming the seventh Doctor Who in 1987. Since his retirement from *Doctor Who* in 1989, he has continued to work on stage and TV and in movies.

Sylvester actually met Peter Jackson in Wellington in 2007. He had been in The Royal Shakespeare Company's production of *King Lear* and Ian McKellen introduced them. Peter was thrilled because he is a big *Doctor Who* fan.

When Sylvester McCoy was cast as Radagast fans were surprised. Superfan Quickbeam wrote in an article for TheOneRing.net: 'I am very excited by what Sylvester McCoy may bring to the role. The rumours are strongly suggesting Radagast's rustic home on the eaves of Mirkwood Forest – Rhosgobel – will be more heavily featured than first suspected.

'Colour me intrigued! This kind of "newly added" material in Peter Jackson's film adaptation is not canonical, strictly speaking, within the pages of *The Hobbit*. Yet it is canon from another Tolkien book! This stuff comes from the Appendices in the hinterlands of *The Return of the King*, and therefore the most intriguing as to how it'll play out in the new films. Among purists it might be cause for alarm.'

> **DID YOU KNOW?**
> Sylvester McCoy tries to play the spoons in every movie he acts in, much to the delight of his fans who find it really funny.

Roäc

- Name: Roäc
- Alias: None
- Race: Raven
- Played by: Likely to be CGI (computer generated imagery). Voice not confirmed
- Character description: Roäc is an ancient raven, who is going blind and struggles to fly. His father was called Carc, and he was living on the Lonely Mountain when Smaug first arrived. He stayed there with his wife and Roäc was born eighteen years later.

  Roäc is a friend of the dwarves and communicates with Dain before the Battle of Five Armies. He was the one who told Thorin and the dwarves that Smaug had been killed. He also warned them that elves and lake men were on their way to claim a share of the treasure.

S

Saruman

- Name: Saruman
- Alias: Saruman the White, Curunír ('Man of Craft/Skill'), Curumo, White Messenger, Saruman of Many Colours, Sharkey or Sharkû ('Old Man')
- Race: Maiar/Istari/Ithryn
- Played by: Christopher Lee
- Character description: Saruman is not mentioned by name in *The Hobbit*. He is very tall, with raven hair in Tolkien's *Unfinished Tales*, and in *The Lord of the Rings* he is described as being an old man with mainly white hair.

The actor chosen to play Saruman in *The Hobbit* and *The Lord of the Rings* movies was Sir Christopher Lee. He was born on 27 May 1922 in Belgravia, London, which made him the oldest member of the cast.

After leaving school, he worked as an office clerk but in 1941 enlisted in the RAF during World War II. He left the RAF in 1947 and became a member of the Rank Organisation, a British entertainment company. It was the biggest film company in the UK, set up by an industrialist called J. Arthur Rank. To begin with, he received training and then started acting in Rank movies, playing small roles in *Corridor of Mirrors*, *Hamlet*, *One Night with You* and *A Song for Tomorrow*.

Christopher Lee became a popular actor in the 1950s when he began working with Hammer Film Productions, playing Creature in *The Curse of Frankenstein*, Count Dracula in *Horror of Dracula*, Kharis/The Mummy in *The Mummy* and Sir Henry in *The Hound of the Baskervilles*, to name but a few. He was a great horror actor but by the late 1970s he was turning his hand to a wide variety of roles because he didn't want to be pigeonholed.

Over the years he has become one of Britain's best-loved actors and has appeared in 275 movies, making him a Guinness World Record holder. He is best known for playing Dracula, Francisco Scaramanga in the James Bond movie *The Man with the Golden Gun* and Count Dooku/ Darth Tyranus in *Star Wars: Episode II – Attack of the Clones*. In 2001, he was given an OBE by the Queen for his contribution to the movie and television industries.

Because Sir Christopher is ninety years old, he has naturally slowed down a lot and only does jobs he really wants to do. Also, he only plays parts requiring a few days' work otherwise he gets exhausted. He was keen to play Saruman in *The Hobbit* movies but couldn't travel all the way to New Zealand so instead shot his scenes for both films over four days in London. In his Christmas 2011 video to fans he spoke of his wish to live to see the movies when they came out. He also reminded them that the Saruman in *The Hobbit* is 'a good and noble man and the head of the Council of Wizards, as he had always been.'

DID YOU KNOW?

Christopher Lee is the only person in *The Lord of the Rings/ The Hobbit* cast who knew Tolkien personally. He is considered an expert on the books and used to read them every year.

To find out more about Christopher Lee, visit his official website: ww.christopherleeweb.com.

Scale Doubles

Lots of scale doubles were used in *The Hobbit* movies: scale doubles were needed for Bilbo, the dwarves, Gandalf and many of the other characters because of the enormous size differences between different species. A big moment for the actors who play the dwarves was when they all tried their costumes on for the first time and lined up for a photograph. In front of them were their scale doubles: they looked virtually identical, just smaller.

One of *The Hobbit* scale doubles was Kiran Shah, a scale double, actor and stuntman. In *The Lord of the Rings* movies he was Elijah Wood's scale double, playing Frodo. He is a Guinness World Record holder, with his entry stating that he is the 'Shortest Professional Stuntman currently working in film'. In *The Hobbit* movies he is Martin Freeman's (Bilbo's) scale double and plays a goblin, too. Previously, he has worked on *Raiders of the Lost Ark*, *Star Wars: Episode VI – Return of the Jedi*, *Ridley Scott's Legend* and *The Chronicles of Narnia: The Lion, the Witch and the Wardrobe*.

Another of the scale doubles was Brett Beattie. He was Dean O'Gorman's (Fili's) scale double and had been John Rhys-Davies' (Gimli's) scale double in *The Lord of the Rings* movies. Brett had been the one who got the tattoo with the main Fellowship actors. In a forum post on the red-carpet Fellowship page in 2006 he wrote: 'A warm gidday from Brett Beattie from the beautiful South Island of New Zealand – for anyone who is wondering who the hell I am, I was the sucker who spent 189 days in a heavy silicon prosthetic mask, dacron fatsuit and 20 kgs of costume, armour and weapons as Gimli, doubling for John Rhys-Davies. I choreographed and performed Gimli's fighting, stunts and the dodgy horse work involved. I also had to learn Gimli's script most days for voiceovers.

'It is a known fact that I spent more time on set and film than the credited actor John Rhys-Davies. I'm only 4 ft 10" – which is how they managed to create the scale illusion of Gimli. My hard work didn't go unnoticed and at the end of filming I was invited by the main cast to join them in receiving one of the nine elven tattoos for Gimli.

'I guess one of the finest moments while working on the Rings Trilogies (apart from receiving my elven tattoo) was my final Gimli prosthetic application. I was so over the glues and solvents taking layers of skin off my face day after day. It was a huge relief knowing I had completed such a hardcore feat and got through it, without too many of my marbles rolling away!'

He must have enjoyed himself to sign up for *The Hobbit* movies!

At the opposite end of the scale doubles was Paul Randall. Paul's nickname among the cast and crew is 'Tall Paul' as he's 7' 1" tall. He was Sir Ian McKellen's scale double, playing Gandalf; he was also his scale double in *The Lord of the Rings* movies. Dressed up in Gandalf's robes, with his beard and hat he looks exactly like him and his movements are just the same as when Ian McKellen is playing him because he has been fully trained by Sir Ian and the scale doubles movement coach, Nick Blake.

The male scale doubles were between 4' and 5' 2" or 6' 8" or taller, while the female scale doubles were between 4' and 5'.

DID YOU KNOW?

While filming *The Lord of the Rings: The Two Towers*, Sean Astin (who played Samwise Gamgee) directed a short film featuring Paul Randall. It was shot on their day off in Wellington and involved other members of the cast and crew. *The Long and Short of It* is well worth a watch. Cinematographer Andrew Lesnie played the painter character and the small woman who comes to his rescue is played by Praphaphorn Chansantor, a scale double for Pippin in *The Lord of the Rings* movies. Director Peter Jackson even appeared as a bus driver to whisk them all away!

Scriptwriters

The scripts for *The Hobbit* movies were written by director Peter Jackson, Philippa Boyens, Fran Walsh and Guillermo del Toro. Previously, Peter, Philippa and Fran had written *The Lord of the Rings* scripts together, as well as scripts for *King Kong* and *The Lovely Bones*. As mentioned earlier, Peter and Fran are married and Fran co-wrote all his screenplays apart from his first movie, *Bad Taste* (1987). Fran had written the screenplay *Worzel Gummidge Down Under* prior to working on her first screenplay with Peter: *Meet the Feebles* (1989).

DID YOU KNOW?

Philippa Boyens was a playwright before she began writing the first *The Lord of the Rings* script.

In February 2010, Peter Jackson admitted to journalist Rob Carnevale: 'Really, my favourite part of the whole process of filmmaking is the screenplay – that's the part that is less pressured, it's the most creative, it's the most freedom and it's fun.'

The team began writing in August 2008. Peter, Fran and Philippa worked in New Zealand, but Guillermo was still living in Los Angeles, California and so they had to videoconference each other. They had face-to-face meetings every three weeks because Guillermo would fly to New Zealand especially (his flights were 13 or so hours each way). Jackson summed up what writing as a team is like in a Weta webchat. He said: 'Writing a screenplay with a group of collaborators is like the Lennon McCartney collaboration. Sometimes one or two people do more than others on certain parts of the process and vice versa, it all comes out in the wash and we share equal credit in what everyone has done, with four of us we will be able to divide the work up in interesting ways and everyone will be able to help craft these films.'

Del Toro used to plan his days so that in the mornings he would write and then in the afternoons he would research Tolkien. He felt it was vital that he understood what Tolkien was trying to do in *The Hobbit* and he felt a lot of it came from the author's experiences of World War I. Guillermo read lots of books, watched numerous documentaries and consulted with Peter Jackson, who is a collector of all things World War I. He revealed to *New Yorker* journalist Daniel Zalewski: 'Peter Jackson is such a fan of that historical moment and obsessive collector of World War I memorabilia, and he owns several genuine, life-size working reproductions of planes, tanks, cannons, ships! He has the perfect obsessive reproductions of uniforms of that time for armies of about 120 soldiers each. I asked him which books he recommended because I wouldn't be watching *Krull* or *The Dark Crystal* – I need to find my OWN way into the story. That's the same way I did *Pan's Labyrinth* or *Devil's Backbone*, by watching stuff you wouldn't think about.'

After writing for four months, Guillermo told Comingsoon.net: 'Literally, like every week, what you discover writing the two movies, writing the two stories, it changes. So, every week there's a discovery, and anything we say this week would be contradicted next week. Certainly that would be true in casting. Why create hopes or why create expectations if down the line you're going to go, "You know what? That was not a good idea." '

By January 2009, Guillermo and the rest of the writing team were spending twelve hours a day crafting the scripts and he would then have a meeting with Weta Workshop and Weta Digital to go through the designs of various things. The studios signed off the movie treatments and storylines in March 2009 so the writing team then had to come up with the two finished screenplays, no easy task. At this point Guillermo planned to direct every scene but Peter didn't think this was realistic and offered to be the second unit director. During an online chat with fans, Jackson explained: 'Most directors prefer to direct everything themselves. I thought I could on *LOTR*, but very quickly found out that the sheer scale prevented it. Instead of a 15-month shoot, we would have shot for three years! Guillermo always shoots his own material, so we'll do our best to construct a schedule that allows him to do that. It will depend a lot on how the scripts break down. I'd happily shoot some second unit stuff anytime Guillermo asked me to, but let's see what happens.'

In July 2009, Peter revealed during ComicCon: 'We're about three or four weeks away from delivering our first draft of the first *Hobbit* script to Warner Brothers. People assume that we have a green light, that we're making the movie: we don't. We have to deliver the script, the studio obviously has to approve the script and then we have to budget the script because we have no budget yet, so you know, they're not going to make the film with an open cheque book so we have to figure out how much it's going to cost and if that's going to be OK. So that's the process to go through.'

Back then Guillermo del Toro was the director and he talked to Rotten Tomatoes about the weight of expectation for *The Hobbit* on his back. He said: 'I feel very comfortable with it technically, I feel very comfortable with it creatively. The writing I'm partnering up with people I absolutely admire – Philippa, Fran and Peter. When you watch *The Lord of the Rings* movies, which I have done recently many, many times, you realise the quality, the human and emotional quality of the writing is superb in my book.'

Peter and Philippa have given numerous interviews

over the years but Fran is much more private. When asked by journalist Nina Rehfeld from Green Cine why she never takes part in interviews, Peter replied: 'Well, she does that of her own choice. She's my partner and when we try to take our kids to the movies, she sees the difficult time that I have going to the movies in New Zealand, where I get stopped all the time. People want to talk to me and have autographs, which is nice but Fran has determined that she never wants to become a familiar face or a celebrity in that way.'

Once the scriptwriting team were happy with the script, this wasn't the end as they let the actors have a say during their initial rehearsal; they wanted to know if there was anything they could add to make it better. Ian McKellen wrote about what happened that day in his website's official blog: 'I was in an old paint factory, which I knew ten years back as the main film studio for *The Lord of the Rings*. Inside was the new set for Bag End, including a bedroom and pantry.

'And I was there too, in Hobbiton, with a semi-circle of dwarves and Bilbo, their reluctant host. I was at the cast's first joint rehearsal where Peter Jackson, with Fran Walsh and Philippa Boyens, invited our comments on their script so far. This is as close to bliss as an actor can get. Facing three Oscar-winning screenplay writers who genuinely want us actors to contribute. AND there were piles of snacks on the coffee tables: fresh fruit, NZ cheese, Minties.

'Two of the cast have forsworn desserts during Lent. Not me, not yet. At lunch I took seconds of the flourless chocolate cake and sour cream.'

Peter Jackson explained to fans how the writing process works through a Facebook post he did on Thursday, 21 April 2011. He explained that there are three distinct phases in the life of a film script. The first phase is the script before filming has started, the second phase happens once the actors start sharing their thoughts and filming starts. The third phase happens once filming finishes, in post-production. His favourite phase is phase two. 'Sometimes we have gotten these revisions to the actors a little late,' he wrote. 'We constantly joke to Ian McKellen that tomorrow's script pages will be slid under his door sometime the night before and sometimes that has been true.'

Smaug the Dragon

- Name: Smaug
- Alias: Smaug the Magnificent, Golden, Lord Smaug the Impenetrable, the Dragon, Tremendous, Chiefest and Greatest of Calamaties, Mighty, The Monster, Old Worm, Worm of Dread

- Race: Dragon (Fire-drake)
- Played by: Likely to be CGI (computer generated imagery), with the voice of Benedict Cumberbatch
- Character description: Smaug is a dragon who is red and gold in colour. He enjoys killing dwarves and any other creatures he can and lives in the Misty Mountains, surrounded by his treasure.

The actor chosen to voice Smaug was Benedict Cumberbatch, a British actor who was born in London. He is best known for playing Sherlock Holmes in the BBC drama *Sherlock* and for his role as Stephen Hawking in the BBC drama *Hawking*.

While Guillermo del Toro was directing the movie, he told *New Yorker* journalist Daniel Zalewski: 'All my life I've been fascinated by dragons. I was born under the Chinese sign of The Dragon. All my life I'm collecting dragons. It's such a powerful symbol, and in the context of *The Hobbit*, it is used to cast its shadow through the entire narrative. Essentially, Smaug represents so many things: greed, pride, he's "the Magnificent", after all. The way his shadow is cast in the narrative you cannot then show it and have it be one thing, he has to be the embodiment of all those things. He's one of the few dragons that will have enormous scenes with lines. He has some of the most beautiful dialogues in those scenes! The design, I'm pretty sure that will be the last design we will sign off on, and the first design we have attempted. It is certainly a matter of turning every stone before figuring out what he looks like, because what he looks like will tell you what he is.'

DID YOU KNOW?

The fact that Benedict Cumberbatch had been cast in *The Hobbit* was supposed to be a secret but Martin Freeman accidentally mentioned it at the 2011 BAFTAs (BAFTA stands for British Academy of Film and Television Arts). Sir Ian McKellen then wrote on his blog: 'The cat is out of the bag. The actor is named. The latest recruit to the Jackson troops is the superb Benedict Cumberbatch, Sherlock Holmes to Bilbo's Watson.'

Cumberbatch chatted to *MTV News* about working with Peter Jackson and Martin Freeman (who plays Watson in *Sherlock*, as well as Bilbo in *The Hobbit*). He admitted: 'I was very lucky [to work] with Pete. As far as the experience, what an extraordinary one it was because at the time I was in my work; I was in isolation with him and this incredible tag team. And at the very cool place with that technology doing mo-cap for two characters, Smaug the dragon and another character, which will remain nameless, and it was an awful lot of fun.'

The other character Benedict plays, whom he refused to name in the *MTV News* interview was Necromancer (who ends up being Sauron). In a separate interview with *Empire* magazine he said that Necromancer is a character from the *Five Legions War* that Peter Jackson wanted to put in *The Hobbit* movies. He actually annoyed many Tolkien fans by saying *Five Legions War* when he should have said *Battle of Five Armies* but *Sherlock* fans forgave him because he is only human and must have been confused.

Benedict didn't get to spend that much time on set because he was mainly doing voice work, but he did see Martin Freeman in his Bilbo costume. He found it so funny: 'It was great. I got to hang out with him, and I kept a straight face for a bit and then I started giggling because I know Martin, I don't know Bilbo. For Martin to be sitting there, playing Bilbo is amazing. He's going to be amazing; he's going to be fantastic in this film!'

FILM FACT

In April 2011 *Forbes* magazine ranked Smaug as the richest fictional character.

Here is the Top Ten:
• Smaug: $62 Billion
• Flintheart Glomgold: $51.9 Billion

- Carlisle Cullen: $36.3 Billion
- Jed Clampett: $9.8 Billion
- Tony Stark: $9.3 Billion
- Richie Rich: $8.9 Billion
- Charles Foster Kane: $8.3 Billion
- Bruce Wayne: $6.9 Billion
- Forrest Gump: $5.7 Billion
- Mr Monopoly: $2.5 Billion

Spiders

- Name: Spiders
- Alias: Attercop, Tomnoddy, Lazy Lob, Crazy Cob
- Race: Spider
- Played by: Likely to be CGI (computer generated imagery)
- Character description: The spiders are huge beasts with large bodies the size of footballs and big, hairy legs. They view the dwarves and Bilbo as meat.

DID YOU KNOW?

Tolkien decided to include spiders in *The Hobbit* because his son Michael hated them.

When Guillermo del Toro was the director he had a

meeting with Weta Workshop and the design team to come up with the concept of how the spiders should look (he didn't want them to look identical to Shelob in *The Lord of the Rings* movies).

Stuntmen

There were lots of stuntmen needed for *The Hobbit* movies, especially in the battle scenes. One of the stuntmen was 6' 9" basketball star Mike Homik, who played for the Manawatu Jets at the time of shooting. Homik had never been a stuntman before but enjoyed himself so much that he decided to retire from basketball so he could concentrate on carving out a career as a stuntman in movies.

He told reporter George Heagney from Stuff.co.nz: 'It's quite sad thinking about hanging up the boots and looking back, because it's been my life – basketball, the last 17 years. Every day up until *The Hobbit*.'

Previously he had spoken with Heagney in February 2012 to tell him what it was like to be a stuntman. He revealed: 'What we do here on *The Hobbit* is mostly fighting or falling off something. It's fun. It's like being a really big kid, but a bit more professional.'

Like many of *The Hobbit* stuntmen and women, Mike is trained in martial arts. He has experience of karate, Taekwondo and Muay Thai (a martial art similar to kickboxing).

A lot of the other main stunt doubles had worked together before on *The Lord of the Rings* movies, *Yogi Bear*, *King Kong*, *Avatar*, *The Adventures of Tintin* and *Spartacus*.

Here is a list of the dwarf stunt doubles:
- Allan Smith (Jed Brophy/Nori)
- Bronson Steel (Steven Hunter/Bombur)
- David J. Muzzeral (Adam Brown/Ori)
- Isaac Hammon (John Callen/Oin)
- James Waterhouse-Brown (Dean O'Gorman/ Fili)
- Jeremy Hollis (Mark Hadlow/Dori)
- Mana Davis (Richard Armitage/Thorin)
- Peter Dillon (Ken Stott/Balin)
- Sean Button (Aiden Turner/Kili)
- Scott Chiplin (William Kircher/Bifur)
- Tony Marsh (Peter Hambleton/Glóin)
- Vincent Roxburgh (James Nesbitt/Bofur)
- Winham Hammond (Graham McTavish/Dwalin)

Tauriel

- Name: Tauriel ('Woodland Daughter')
- Alias: None
- Race: Silvan Elf of Mirkwood
- Played by: Evangeline Lilly
- Character description: Tauriel does not appear in *The Hobbit* book. She was created especially for the movies and is the head of the Elven guard. A strong fighter, she can use a bow or daggers to kill her enemies.

The actress chosen to play Tauriel was Evangeline Lilly, a Canadian who now lives in Hawaii. She is best known for playing Kate Austen in the TV drama *Lost*, and dated Dominic Monaghan for five years before they split in 2009 (Dominic played Meriadoc Brandybuck in *The Lord of the Rings* movies). She told Access Hollywood: 'My character is an invention of Peter Jackson and Fran Walsh so, either fans are going to love her or absolutely despise and be bitter towards her because she's not authentic.

'I believe she is authentic because Tolkien refers to The Wooded Owls – he just doesn't talk about who they are specifically. [Peter and Fran] know that world so well. They're not going to create a character that is not true to Tolkien's world.'

Peter Jackson announced her casting via his Facebook page. He wrote: 'Evangeline Lilly will be playing a new character – the Woodland Elf, Tauriel. Her name means "Daughter of Mirkwood" and, beyond that, we must leave you guessing! (No, there is no romantic connection to Legolas.) What is not a secret is how talented and compelling an actress Evangeline is; we are thrilled and excited she will be the one to bring our first true Sylvan Elf to life.'

Evangeline is a massive Tolkien fan and when the first *The Lord of the Rings* movie came out in 2001, she resisted going to see it because she didn't think it would do the book justice. She confessed to Reelz.com: 'I thought it was sacrilege that anyone would adapt Tolkien's work. I didn't think anyone would justify films by making them as good as they should be. Then my entire family when I was visiting went to see the movie and so I relented and went. We were all fans of the books and we were all blown away! It was a little piece of magic what Peter Jackson accomplished because it was truly a homage to the books rather than an offense.'

Being such a big fan of Tolkien's books, Evangeline expected negative feedback from fans because she would be playing a new character. She admitted, back in September 2011: 'I am very concerned to this day that people will watch the film and I'll be the black mark on the film. I know how adamant the purists are and I'm one of them! That said, upon reading *The Hobbit* again, as an adult, I can see why additional characters were needed to round out the story as an adaptation – especially female characters! *The Hobbit* didn't include female characters at all and was a very linear story, a book for children, really. What Peter, Fran and Philippa have done is all in perfect keeping with Tolkien's world, while adding a third dimension to an otherwise very two-dimensional story.'

Back in January 2012, she chatted to Yahoo Movies about how she prepared to play Tauriel. Evangeline explained: '[Usually] I'm a fairly spontaneous actor, I like to keep things fresh and real and alive. And therefore, I don't do a lot of prepping.' However, she had to change the way she does things when it came to playing Tauriel: 'I can't just be spontaneous because there is nothing natural about being an elf. It's not human, so I have to study to learn what it means to be this other creature. So, on top of my stunt training, which I need to learn how to be proficient with the bow and arrow, and with daggers, and in fighting orcs that are, you know, ten feet tall, I also have to learn the language of Elvish and I have to learn an RP [Received Pronunciation] neutral English accent for when I speak English.'

Thranduil, the Elvenking

• Name: Elvenking, Thranduil
• Alias: Woodland King
• Race: Sindarin Elf
• Played by: Lee Pace
• Character description: The Elvenking wears a crown of red leaves and berries in the autumn months and carries a staff of oak.

The actor chosen to play the Elvenking was American Lee Pace. Lee was born in Chickasha, Oklahoma, but grew up in Saudi Arabia before returning to the USA for his teenage years. He started acting at high school and was so sure that he wanted to be a professional actor that he dropped out, choosing to perform at his local Alley Theatre instead. Realising he needed to get his qualifications, he returned for exams and then got at a place at Juilliard Drama Division so he could learn the necessary skills to become a successful actor.

After graduating, he worked off-Broadway, starring in *The Credeaux Canvas* and *The Fourth Sister*. He continued to work in the theatre but in 2003 was cast as Calpernia Addams/Scottie in the movie, *Soldier's Girl*. After impressing critics and audiences with his performance, he won a Gotham Award for Outstanding Breakthrough Performance. He was also nominated for Golden Globes and the Independent Spirit Award, but missed out.

Lee has continued to act on the stage, in movies and in television dramas. He is best known for playing the lead character Ned in the comedy drama *Pushing Daisies* (2007–09), which also starred Anna Friel and Kristin Chenoweth.

Director Peter Jackson announced the casting on his Facebook page, telling fans: 'I'm also pleased to announce that Lee Pace will be playing the Elven King Thranduil. Casting these Tolkien stories is very difficult, especially the Elven characters, and Lee has always been our first choice for Thranduil. He's going to be great. We loved his performance in a movie called *The Fall* a few years ago, and have been hoping to work with him since. When we were first discussing who would be right for Thranduil, Lee came into mind almost immediately.'

Thorin Oakenshield

- Name: Thorin
- Alias: Oakenshield, King Under the Mountain, King of Durin's Folk in Exile
- Race: Dwarf, House of Durin
- Played by: Richard Armitage
- Character description: Thorin is a born leader, strong and courageous. He wants to claim back The Lonely Mountain and its treasure from Smaug.

The actor chosen to play Thorin in *The Hobbit* movies was Richard Armitage. In the animated 1977 version he was voiced by Hans Conried.

FILM FACT:

When Guillermo del Toro was the director he had approached Brian Blessed as a potential Thorin. Blessed is a British actor best known for his deep, booming voice. He played Lord Locksley in the 1991 movie *Robin Hood* and Richard IV in the first series of *The Black Adder* (1983).

Richard Armitage was born in Leicester, England and knew from a young age that he wanted to be an actor. He revealed to the *Metro*: 'I read *The Lord of the Rings* about five times as a young kid. I had this dream of getting on a horse and doing all that stuff. Then I went to college and we went regularly to see the Royal Shakespeare Company. I saw *A Midsummer Night's Dream* and *The Taming of the Shrew*. I remember understanding Shakespeare for the first time and really laughing at it, and I thought that's the kind of thing I wanted to do.

'I went into musical theatre, which I'm not really cut out for – I'm not as skilled at it as other people. There were open auditions advertised in *The Stage*, where you'd turn up with 3,000 other people. You'd queue, do your song and bugger off. I decided I was in the wrong field, went back to drama school and went through the process again but for more dramatic jobs and got into the RSC. The first ten years were quite a struggle.'

DID YOU KNOW?

When Richard was seventeen he joined a circus for six months so he could get his Equity Card. His job was holding ladders for the trapeze artists and passing batons to the jugglers. In the past, he has also worked as an usher in a theatre and as an estate agent.

Armitage got his first big TV job in 2002 in the BBC drama *Sparkhouse* and has been in dozens of TV series since then. He is best known for playing Sir Guy of Gisborne in the *Robin Hood* TV series and Lucas North in *Spooks*. Also, he was the love interest (and later husband) of Geraldine Granger in the British sitcom, *The Vicar of Dibley*. He thinks he usually ends up playing the bad guy roles because of the way he looks, telling the *Telegraph*: 'I suppose I'm a bit mean. My face on camera doesn't lend itself to happy nice guys. I think it's just that my bone structure looks menacing – I don't smile that often.'

Richard has appeared in several movies, from the thriller *Frozen* to the superhero movie *Captain America: The First Avenger*, but *The Hobbit* films will be the biggest he has ever been in. He can remember reading the book as a child quite a few times but found it interesting re-reading it as a man.

Initially, some Tolkien fans objected to Armitage being cast as Thorin, with one fan nicknamed Moif writing on a FirstShowing.net comment board: 'The images of the dwarves released so far do not correspond to the descriptions in the book, and Thorin Oakenshield is supposed to be very old. This image does not look anything like the description of Thorin Oakenshield.'

Another fan called Kraeten added: 'It's one thing to

make one of the background dwarves look like a young human that happens to be short. It's another thing entirely to screw up the most important dwarf in *The Hobbit*.'

Director Peter Jackson decided to defend Armitage in an interview with *Entertainment Weekly*. He said: 'Thorin Oakenshield is a tough, heroic character, and he certainly should give Leggie [Legolas] and Aragorn a run for their money in the heartthrob stakes – despite being four feet tall.

'In Middle-earth, dwarves are a noble race and have a culture and physical appearance which sets them apart from humans. It's fun to develop these different cultures for the movie, and we are doing much more with dwarves this time around than we did with Gimli in Lord of the Rings.

'Our company of thirteen dwarves in *The Hobbit* lets us explore many different personalities – and costume and make-up designs will support the type of character each actor plays. Richard is a powerful actor with a wide range, and we're very excited to be handing Thorin over to him. In this partnership, we need Richard to give us his depth, range, and emotion as an actor – and we'll make him look like a dwarf!'

Really, the fans weren't objecting to Armitage because of his acting ability but because they felt he was much too young to play the part of Thorin.

DID YOU KNOW?

Richard absolutely hates water and so he doesn't usually go in the sea or go swimming unless he really has to.

In a press conference for *The Hobbit* in New Zealand, Armitage was asked by one journalist why he was suited to the role. He replied: 'That's a good question, actually. I think that might be one for Peter, Fran and Philippa. I just think it's a really amazing opportunity to take a character from a book that I was brought to as a child. My first experience on stage was in a production of *The Hobbit* at the Alex Theatre in Birmingham and I played an elf, and Gollum was a little papier mâché puppet with a man on stage on a microphone. It was in my childhood very prominently. So to come to it as an adult, you know a middle-aged man, and kind of had another look at it is a brilliant opportunity.'

FILM FACT:

Armitage and the other dwarf actors were taught how to speak the dwarf language Khuzdul so they could shout out during the battle scenes.

Richard will never forget his time on *The Hobbit* and he doesn't think he'll ever be able to leave Thorin behind. He told MTV: 'I don't think it will be possible to leave it behind me – I think this is one of those characters that always stay with you because you spend so much time with him and it's such a transformation. I'm in the character every day, and I've become so familiar with him. I sort of know how he thinks. I feel really close to the character, and he will continue beyond this job. I think he is a fascinating character. I will probably wake up in six years' time and be inspired to think about him again. It's really exciting.'

Thráin

- Name: Thráin
- Alias: Heir of Durin, King of Durin's Folk
- Race: Dwarf, House of Durin
- Played by: Mike Mizrahi
- Character description: Thráin was the father of Thorin. He managed to survive Smaug's attack with his father Thrór, thanks to a private side-door that only they knew about. Thráin lost an eye during the Battle of Nanduhirion.

The actor chosen to play Thráin was Mike Mizrahi. Mike

is from New Zealand and has been acting in TV shows and movies since 1989. He played Castor/Ratface in *Hercules: The Legendary Journeys* TV series (1995–96), but playing Thráin is his big break.

Thrór

- Name: Thrór
- Alias: King Under the Mountain
- Race: Dwarf of the House of Durin
- Played by: Jeffrey Thomas
- Character description: Thrór was the father of Thráin and the grandfather of Thorin. King Thrór was a wealthy dwarf until Smaug came along. After escaping with his son, he made a map of the Lonely Mountain.

The actor chosen to play Thrór was Jeffrey Thomas. Born in Wales, he has spent most of his adult life in New Zealand. He studied at both Liverpool and Oxford Universities and is a keen writer of books, plays and scripts.

Thomas is best known for his roles on New Zealand television, playing Inspector Sharky in the police drama *Shark in the Park* and starring in the soap operas *Shortland Street* and *Mercy Peak*. Like several members of *The Hobbit* cast, he was in *Hercules: The Legendary Journeys*, a TV series filmed in New Zealand and America.

He had worked with Peter Jackson before in the mockumentary *Forgotten Silver*, which was released in 1995.

Tom

- Name: Tom
- Alias: Booby
- Race: Stone-troll
- Played by: Likely to be CGI (computer generated imagery). Voice not yet cast
- Character description: Tom, Bert and William are stone-trolls so turn to stone in the daylight.

Richard Armitage (Thorin) was so excited when he saw the stone-trolls because they looked identical to the ones in *The Lord of the Rings* and it made him feel as if he was in *The Lord of the Rings* and not *The Hobbit*!

Unexpected Journey

The decision was made to make two *Hobbit* movies rather than trying to compress everything into one. *An Unexpected Journey* was to be the first and would be released in December 2012. The second was to be called *There and Back Again* and would be hitting cinemas in December 2013. It was later decided that there would be three movies – *The Hobbit: An Unexpected Journey* (December 2012), *The Hobbit: The Desolation of Smaug* (December 2013) and *The Hobbit: There and Back Again* (summer 2014).

For the original director Guillermo del Toro and

eventual director Peter Jackson, creating a consistency between *The Lord of the Rings* and *The Hobbit* movies was important but they also wanted *The Hobbit* films to stand on their own. They expressed as much to fans in an online chat on the Weta website. Del Toro said: 'I believe that it's a little bit of both – the world must feel like the same world. The aspect ratio, music, essential established costume and production design trademarks but I would love to bring a lot of new flavours to the table. *The Hobbit* is, in essence, an overture to a massive Symphonic work, so main themes are reprised but new modulations and new colors are introduced, thematically and texturally.'

Jackson commented: 'I love Guillermo's symphonic allusion. The "overture" can have a different flavour, a different texture, yet be a carefully crafted introduction to what's to follow. Film Two is perfect to dramatise the shift in Middle-earth that propels us into the dark days of *Lord of the Rings*. If *Lord of the Rings* is World War I, then *The Hobbit* is like an Edwardian adventure tale, set in the days before [the] world notices the looming storm clouds.'

On 14 December 2011, Warner Brothers issued a press release. In it they stated that the events of *The Hobbit* occur 60 years before *The Lord of the Rings* and they then gave the following plot summary for the first movie: 'The adventure follows the journey of title character Bilbo Baggins, who is swept into an epic quest to reclaim the lost Dwarf Kingdom of Erebor from the fearsome dragon Smaug. Approached out of the blue by the wizard Gandalf the Grey, Bilbo finds himself joining a company of thirteen dwarves led by the legendary warrior, Thorin Oakenshield. Their journey will take them into the Wild; through treacherous lands swarming with Goblins and Orcs, deadly Wargs and Giant Spiders, Shapeshifters and Sorcerers.'

Originally, the movies were to be directed by Guillermo del Toro, but he stepped down due to his scheduling concerns and Peter Jackson took over. Before he left, Guillermo had told Rotten Tomatoes during an interview: 'When Tolkien wrote the book he was not making a prequel and if there are gaps in the logic of the use or the powers of the ring between the first film and the trilogy, they will be the same gaps that Tolkien had writing the book. We'll try to deal with it, but I'm not going to betray the spirit of the book in order to fit the cinematic incarnation.'

The first movie – *The Hobbit: An Unexpected Journey* – was given a release date of 14 December 2012 in the UK, USA and New Zealand but lucky fans in China, Germany, Greece, Hungary, Israel, Netherlands, Portugal, Russia and Singapore got to see it one day early, on 13 December. Fans in Belgium, Denmark, Finland, France, Norway and Sweden were even luckier and saw it two days earlier on 12 December!

In June 2012, Peter Jackson announced the World Premiere for the movie would be held on 28 November at the Embassy Theatre, Wellington. He told *Variety*: 'We cannot think of a more perfect way to send *The Hobbit* off into the world than to celebrate with a huge party here in Wellington, where the journey began.'

Fans couldn't wait to see how Jackson would include the White Council and Dol Guldur in the three movies, as he had revealed in interviews that they would be in more than one scene.

Visual Effects

The visual effects supervisor on *The Hobbit* movies was Eric Saindon from Weta Digital. Weta Digital is a visual effects company from Wellington, New Zealand and they have worked on huge blockbusters such as *Avatar*, *X-Men First Class*, *Enchanted* and *The A-Team*, as well as Peter Jackson's movies *Tintin*, *The Lovely Bones* and *The Lord of the Rings*. The company was actually founded in 1993 by Peter, Richard Taylor and Jamie Selkirk.

During shooting, Jackson relies a lot on Saindon and will often call over for him. Eric has to photograph every last detail of a prop, set or location so that it can be digitally replicated; he cannot afford to miss a thing so has to concentrate at all times. He has a team of people from Weta Digital to help him: Brian McMillin, Adam Harriman, Seb Abante and Kevin Sherwood. They use a Leica 3D scanning device, which allows them to scan absolutely everything.

Movie critic Eric Vespe from AintItCool.com chatted to Saindon on set and wrote on his set report: 'Eric told me that he can take these high res photos he takes and basically lay them over this framework and have a near photoreal recreation of the shooting area, which makes it easier to roll with digital additions, subtractions and CGI creatures (like Wargs, for instance); that also helps him digitally recreate props to be as close to the physical prop, should he be required to.'

Voice Coaches

One of the voice coaches on *The Hobbit* movies was Leith McPherson, a voice, dialect and acting coach. She relocated to New Zealand so she could be on hand at all times. On her website homepage she left the following message: 'Thanks for dropping by. I'll be away working in New Zealand for much of 2011–2012, although I'll be back in Melbourne mid-year 2011 to team up with Simon Phillips and Ewen Leslie (and William Shakespeare) for *Hamlet* at the

Melbourne Theatre Company. My filming commitments mean it may be difficult to get hold of me, but email will be the best way until I'm back in the country.

'My best regards and I hope you have a wonderful year!'

Leith trained at London's Central School of Speech & Drama. Over the past 14 years she has helped hundreds of actors from all around the world learn how to speak with lots of different accents, too many to list. She has become good friends with several members of *The Hobbit* cast over the last two years. On her Twitter page she describes herself as dialect coach, friend of Elves (@leithmcp). In May 2012, Stephen Fry tweeted: 'Well that was as good a Sunday lunch as I've had for many years. Ah, sweet mystery of Leith... haddock and chips and a good glass of beer.'

W, X, Y, AND Z

William

- Name: William
- Alias: Bill Huggins, Fat Fool, Booby
- Race: Stone-troll
- Played by: Likely to be CGI (computer generated imagery). Voice not yet cast
- Character description: William is the most compassionate of the stone-trolls. He wants Bert and Tom to release Bilbo, but they won't listen and end up fighting over it.

Xbox 360

Peter Jackson is a big fan of video games, thanks to his son Billy, and they play together on their Xbox 360 whenever they get the chance. Jackson was due to be developing an interactive storytelling Xbox 360 game called '*Halo: Chronicles with Microsoft Game Studios*'. In 2006, he built his own video game development studio and called his new company Wingnut Interactive.

Sadly *Halo: Chronicles* was shelved in 2008. Peter told Joystiq.com: 'That *Halo* project is no longer happening; it sort of collapsed when the movie didn't end up happening.'

Journalist Kevin Kelly mentioned that *District 9* would have made a good game, to which Peter replied: 'We definitely felt like *District 9* would have been a great video game property, and both Neill [Blomkamp, the director] and myself love games, but we just couldn't get our heads together. I was working on *The Lovely Bones*, and he was busy filming *District 9*, and we just couldn't get together on it in time.'

Wingnut Interactive are currently working on original games so we'll have to wait and see what filmic Xbox games are released by the studio in the future. Peter revealed in an interview for AintItCool.com: 'I've got ideas that could be a movie or they could be a game and I think that they should, rather than just make a movie and then do a spin-off game. I think some of the ideas I've got, I'd rather do them as a standalone game because that world is getting more and more interesting.'

He also admitted: 'At the moment I am kind of involved with a *Tintin* game and obviously the beginning of *The Hobbit* game, so those two in terms of the gaming at the moment with all of the other scripts we are working on at the moment, those are the gaming things we are focusing on.'

Warner Brothers officially announced in October 2011 that there would be a *Hobbit* video game released before the first movie came out.

YouTube

If you haven't checked out the production videos that Peter took while filming the two movies, you really need to head for YouTube ASAP. Here is the official channel link: www.youtube.com/officialthehobbit. You can also watch the trailers, videos from press conferences and interviews on YouTube.

If you prefer, you can visit the official website instead at www.thehobbit.com. You can download official wallpaper and buddy icons for free on there, or if you want behind-the-scenes news, check out the official blog (www.thehobbitblog.com).

The biggest and best *Hobbit* fan site is TheOneRing.net.

They have the latest movie news and you can chat to other fans on their messageboards.

Zane Weiner

Zane Weiner was one of eight executive producers of *The Hobbit* movies. Director Peter Jackson chose seven other producers to work with him on *The Hobbit*. As well as himself and Weiner, there were Philippa Boyens, Fran Walsh, Carolynne Cunningham, Toby Emmerich, Callum Greene, Alan Horn and Ken Kamins.

Zane worked as a producer on *The Lord of the Rings* movies as well as the Eminem movie *8 Mile*, the Curtis Hanson film *Wonderboys*, and the Disney gorilla movie *Mighty Joe*. He first met Peter back in November 1999 when he moved to New Zealand to work on *The Lord of the Rings* movies.

You would struggle to meet anyone who works harder than Zane as he puts in 18-hour days during shooting. He summed up what his job involves to the *Los Angeles Times*: 'I was brought over to stick with the main unit – Pete's unit. My job was to make sure that what Pete needed was there when he needed it.'

Weiner would start each day at 3.30am, arriving just before the crew so he could do the things he needed to do before filming started. On an average day he would make over 200 phone calls to various people to ensure things ran smoothly and he'd make a lot of toast for the crew.

He confessed to Hugh Hart from the *Los Angeles Times*: 'I checked with the different department heads every day. You stay with the director pretty much all day, taking care of the cast and the crew needs and always prepping for the next day.

'You're dealing with the art department, making sure the sets were ready, dealing with the 45 or so workshop people who were there trimming up the costumes, bringing in all the weapons and prosthetics. You're checking in with the art department, which built over 350 sets, and dealing with all the departments to make sure their equipment was out of the mud and out of the wind.'

When he's not working in New Zealand, Zane lives in Pennsylvania with his wife Niki Harris, who is a director and choreographer.

DID YOU KNOW?

Zane Weiner started out as a stage manager on Broadway.